History Hacking

The Author

History analyst and author Mario Arndt writes about topics you won't find in traditional history books. His analyses of official history reveal how the Middle Ages, the ancient world, and the associated chronologies were fabricated and forged. He has published eight books since 2012.

Website: https://www.HistoryHacking.de/

YouTube Channel in English:
https://www.youtube.com/@HistoryHacking

YouTubeChannel in German:
https://www.youtube.com/@Chronologiekritik

Mario Arndt

History Hacking

English Edition

Production and publishing: BoD - Books on Demand, Norderstedt
ISBN: 9783756821280

Bibliografische Information der Deutschen Nationalbibliothek
Die Deutsche Nationalbibliothek verzeichnet diese Publikation in der Deutschen Nationalbibliografie; detaillierte bibliografische Daten sind im Internet über dnb.d-nb.de abrufbar.

Table of Contents

"It's more fun to be a pirate than to join the Navy." (Steve Jobs)

"ANYTHING GOES"

Paul Feyerabend

Preface

Criticism of the official history and chronology has made a decisive breakthrough since the 1990s. We owe this success to authors like Anatoli Fomenko (e.g., "History: Fiction or Science?"), Gunnar Heinsohn (e.g., "How Old is the Human Race?"), Heribert Illig (e.g., "The Invented Middle Ages"), and Uwe Topper (e.g., "The Great Action").

In the new millennium, this success continued. New authors joined the ranks, such as Christoph Pfister from Switzerland (e.g., "The Matrix of Ancient History") and François de Sarre from France (e.g., "Mais où est donc passé le Moyen Âge?").

The author Mario Arndt became known for the books "The well-structured Middle Ages" (2012) and "The well-structured history" (2015). After that, six more books by him have been published. In this volume the main results of his research are presented.

History Hacking – Anything goes

Forgeries in history

"Forgeries" are a central theme in medieval studies. For example, in 1986 an international congress of the Monumenta Germaniae Historica (Institute for the Study of the Middle Ages) took place. A six-volume conference book with almost 3000 pages was published [MGH 1986].

In the very early Middle Ages, in the Frankish kingdom at the time of the Merovingian dynasty (6th-8th century), already two thirds of all royal charters are considered forgeries. During the subsequent Carolingian dynasty (8th - 10th century) almost half of all royal charters are forgeries, according to the current state of knowledge. The legal historian H. C. Faußner has proved that almost all royal charters before 1122 (Worms Concordat) are forgeries [Faußner 2003].

It is not possible to prove the authenticity of documents that have not yet been proven to be forged. However, they are traditionally referred to as "genuine" until their forgery is proven.

In addition, not all forgeries have been discovered. It is necessary to keep checking whether new fakes can be found.

Furthermore, it was stated: Since it cannot be determined a priori whether the documents really "transmit authentic contents" or not, it is also not possible to "draw conclusions about actual events" from the document contents. Whether they "transmit authentic contents" or not can only be determined by comparing them with already established facts.

Forged documents do not allow any conclusions to be drawn about the circumstances at the time of the forgery unless they are compared with facts that have already been verified. The pretense of false facts is precisely the purpose of a forgery.

There are a multitude of examples of parts of history that were once believed to be true, but are now no longer considered true by official historical scholarship.

Fig. 1: The Donation of Constantine on a fresco from 1246, Sylvester Chapel at the Basilica Santi Quattro Coronati in Rome. Constantine I (Roman emperor from 306-337) donates the western half of the Roman Empire to Pope Sylvester I. The document is a forgery. The document was exposed as a forgery in 1440.

It starts with the creation of the world in the Bible and a whole lot of stories contained in it, continues with the Greek and Roman sagas, about the former fairy-tale kings of the Swedes and Poles before the 10th century, about the failed attempts of Czech nationalists in the 19th century to invent an ancient Czech culture, about the proof of the forgery of so far two thirds of the royal documents from the Merovingian period, up to ecclesiastical forgeries - here the Constantinian Donation is probably best known. And this will go on and on.

Of course, these fabrications and forgeries no longer appear in today's history books, at best as myths, just as Aristotle's physics is no longer taught today. Therefore, many people are not even aware of them.

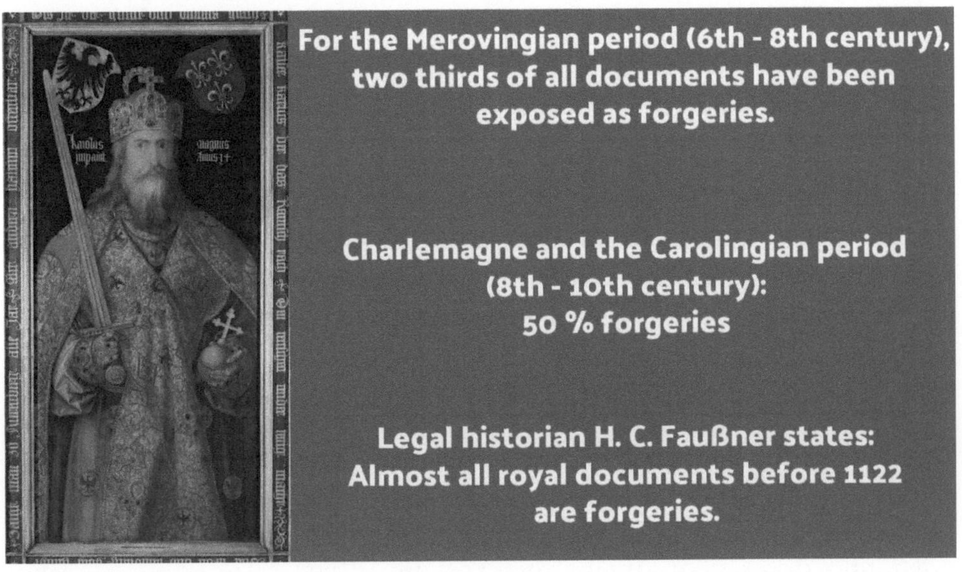

Scientificity in the science of history

Scientificity in itself is no proof of the rightness or wrongness of the objects investigated within the respective science. Rather, the existence of these objects is already presupposed. Therefore, historical science in its current stage of development can only contribute to a limited extent to the understanding of the time before the end of ancient Europe.

This corresponds to the current state of the science of theology, which can also contribute nothing to clarifying the question of whether or not gods and other celestial spirits actually exist.

This can easily be seen in the development of so-called "source criticism" (or information evaluation) over the centuries, for which the starting point was and is "everything is genuine", and not "everything is false" and must first be proven to be genuine.

The objection that a number of written sources from the Middle Ages would prove that the order of kings was as official history teaches, proves on close examination to be a typical argument of closed systems according to the philosopher Karl Raimund Popper (1902-1994), i.e. ultimately a logical fallacy.

With this argument, someone who believes in the accuracy of the content of the Bible, for example, could also prove the creation of the world in six days. The only argument sufficient for the believer is the scriptural source for the creation of the world, the corresponding account in the Bible. He will refute all counter-arguments by claiming that the sources speak against it.

This view of the dogmatists - "All scriptural sources are genuine and what is written in them is true, unless another source speaks against it" - implies an absolute claim to truth that cannot be fulfilled. For that would mean: Everything is automatically true that is written in the written sources. With this methodology, historical science cannot arrive at viable results about the actual distant past.

Dogmatists among historians follow the same pattern. They take the position that the written sources of antiquity and the Middle Ages are all genuine until each one of them is proven to be false.

However, this is not only an inadmissible transfer of today's views on historiography in a small part of the world (claim to objectivity) to past times, but also completely naïve, considering the now already known extent of forgeries.

The description of the creation of the world in the Bible has not been falsified by proving that the text of the Bible is a forgery. One has simply taken a more rational path to knowledge. This is precisely the path of history analysts and critics of chronology.

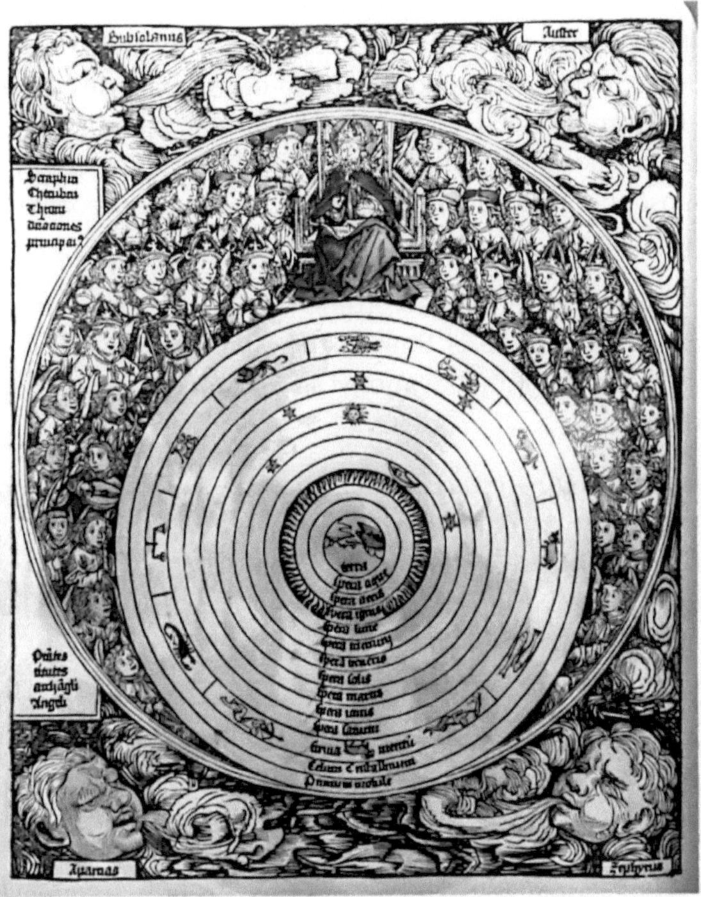

Fig. 3: The geocentric universe, from the "World Chronicle" by Hartmann Schedel (1493)

History according to the geometric method

Fig. 3 shows a medieval (ideal) conception of the universe with the Earth at the centre. The moon, sun and the five planets known at that time (Mercury, Venus, Mars, Jupiter and Saturn) move around the earth in circular orbits. On the very outside are the fixed stars, specifically the twelve constellations of the zodiac.

However, it was known (at least since the ancient astronomer Claudius Ptolemy) that this was not actually true, because the planets were not observed to have exact circular orbits, but rather so-called epicycles (smaller circular orbits on the larger one). Circular orbits were the paradigm of the time, as they were considered the ideal form of motion, as taught by the ancient Greek philosopher and scientist Aristotle. So we see a geometrically idealised representation.

As far as time is concerned, according to Christian understanding, Jesus Christ lives in the middle of time. Is this divine destiny or a symmetrical idealisation based on religious motives? According to the Gospel of Luke, time is divided into

1) The time before Jesus Christ: the law of the Old Testament and the prophets up to John the Baptist,
2) The time of Jesus Christ as the "middle of time",
3) The time between Jesus' ascension and the beginning of the 7th world age.

Jerusalem, where he died on the cross according to the Christian view and where his tomb lies, is in the middle of the world according to the medieval view.

Fig. 4 shows the earth as an ideal conception at that time with Jerusalem in the centre. Here, too, there was a deliberate deviation from reality, as it was of course well known that the coastlines do not follow the ideal so exactly. So this is also a geometrically idealised representation.

Fig. 4: **The earth with Jerusalem at its centre according to medieval, Christian conception**

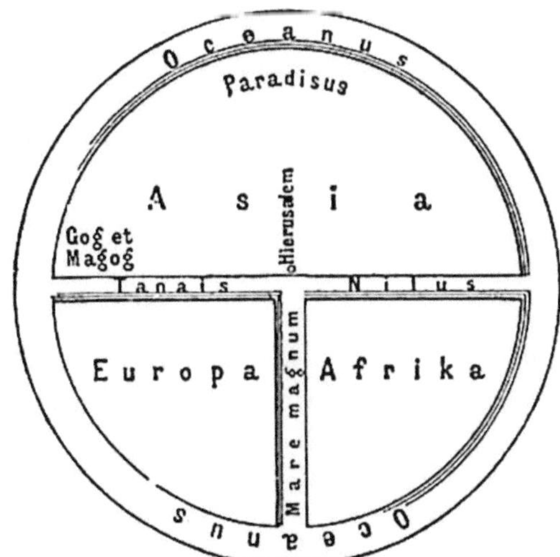

This naturally leads to the assumption that the representation of history in space and time could be the same as in astronomy, chronology and geography. The claim to power of the Christian kings of the Middle Ages was traced back to the creator of the world, God. According to the Christian conception, the (Holy) Roman Empire was regarded as the last world empire before the end of this world.

Therefore, according to the understanding of the time, it is obvious that the order and beauty of God's creation is reflected not only in the universe and on earth, but also in the history of the sons of Adam, and especially in the succession of God-ordained rulers of the Middle Ages.

H.W. Goetz, writing about the historian Otto von Freising and other historiographers of the High Middle Ages, states:

"Time is linear, even though it is constantly up and down. For the historiographer, it brings order to the chaos of history, so to speak. In the medieval view, however, it means finding the given (divine) order.

[...] order, on the other hand, reveals the divine plan. [...]

... but the inquisitive researcher finds - and this is the tenor hystoriae for Otto - "a well-ordered sequence of past events"." [Goetz 1993]

Important factors in structuring the historiography were number symbolism and astrology. In this way, for example, it was determined when the city of Rome was founded. Varro (116 BCE - 27 CE) started from the fall of Troy (1193 BCE according to today's calendar), and calculated the foundation of Rome four saecula of 110 years each, i.e. 440 years later. This was for him the correct time span between death and rebirth according to astrologers. This is the year 753 BCE, which is still commonly used today.

Other examples are the date of the creation of the world or the date of the birth of the Messiah. In the Christian, European Middle Ages, the number-symbolic model was of course the Bible. The example of the "Annolied", a historical poem attributed to the 11th century (first printed in 1639 after the only manuscript that since then has disappeared), shows well how biblically influenced number symbolism structures the story presented. In this work, the numbers 3, 4, 7 and 33 play a special role.

These examples are obviously currently perceived as isolated cases in official history because the full extent is not yet known. But they are not isolated cases, but only typical examples of an idealised construction of God-ordained history according to the laws of geometry in a time with different social and religious circumstances than today.

Geometry has served in the sciences since antiquity as a method of casting everything into a system with ideal and symmetrical forms, even things that were actually unknown. The high point of this rationalist worldview was the 17th century. French gardens with their symmetrical arrangement (ancient Greek συμμετρία = "evenness") illustrate the principle. In philosophy, Baruch Spinoza wrote his well-known "Ethica, ordine geometrico demonstrata" (Latin = Ethics, Demonstrated in Geometrical Order) and the music of Johann Sebastian Bach is characterised by its strict geometrical structure.

In natural philosophy (now natural science), groundbreaking successes were achieved with the geometric method. Ideal concepts of the world were the basis for successful models that explained the world and opened up the unknown.

Johannes Kepler (1571-1630), the discoverer of the three laws of planetary motion, wrote in his book "Harmonices mundi libri V" (Five Books on the Harmonics of the World):

"I feel seized by an inexpressible rapture at the divine spectacle of heavenly harmony. For we see here how God, like a human master builder, has approached the foundation of the world according to order and rule."

Fig. 5: God as (geometer and) creator of the universe in a manuscript from the Middle Ages

Analytics of history as system analysis

"Analytics of history exyplores the historians' models (including chronological ones), looks for errors, contradictions, seeks to correct them, to improve them, creates conditions for a better reconstruction of the past." [Gabowitsch 2008]

The world view at the time of antiquity and the Middle Ages was fundamentally different from today's world view. But official history has adopted the historical constructions of this time without subjecting them to a radical critique, as happened in other sciences at the beginning of the modern era.

The "Copernican turn" is still to come.

The representatives of official history have not yet achieved the "Copernican turn", thus represent a medieval world view as far as history is concerned. And this error is exposed with Analytics of history.

Their views are comparable to the views of astronomers, physicists and biologists before Copernicus, Newton and Darwin.

According to this worldview, regularities, structures and patterns in history would not be an indication or proof of falsification, but evidence of divine order.

What we now regard as impossible coincidence and therefore fabricated, would not have been recognised at all in the past or would have been regarded as evidence of a divine order. This includes a new concept of probability that emerged in the 17th century.

Aristotle still said: Chance fundamentally is beyond human knowledge and science.

The historian Otto von Freising (1112-1158) wrote in his chronicle "Chronica sive historia de duabus civitatibus" ("History of the Two States") of a "salvation-historical plan of God" in history.

The difference between the past and history

"History has a double meaning.
Firstly, it denotes what has happened [...].
Secondly, however, the word also denotes the representation of what has happened, history."

These sentences begin Heinrich Leo's "Lehrbuch der Universalgeschichte" (Textbook of Universal History) from 1839.

History is what historians have found out so far (more precisely: believe they have found out) about the past that actually happened, i.e. what is also taught at universities and schools and what is written in the historians' books. Official history, however, is only a model, an idea of the actual past, not the past itself. The model can, of course, also be wrong.

The past is what actually happened, what the people who lived at that time actually did and experienced.

Knowledge about the past can only be incomplete. The further back the past lies, the more incomplete tends to be the knowledge about those times, which does not exclude the fact that there can also be periods of time about which we are better informed.

Particularly problematic is the period for which the historian Otto Brunner (1898 - 1982) coined the term "Old Europe" ("Alteuropa"), i.e. antiquity, the Middle Ages and the early modern period up to about 1800. What we think we know about these periods, especially about antiquity and the Middle Ages, comes for the most part from reading texts shaped by ideology and literature.

Only to a very small extent do we have knowledge of the supposed facts of this time through testimonies that come from the actions of those living at the time themselves (so-called "remains", "contemporary testimonies"). Here there is a decisive difference to modernity.

The historian F.-J. Schmale describes this as follows

"In the practice of the historical sciences, the historiography of the Middle Ages has therefore been viewed fundamentally differently from the historiography of the modern age, without this being theoretically justified." [Schmale 1985, S.2]

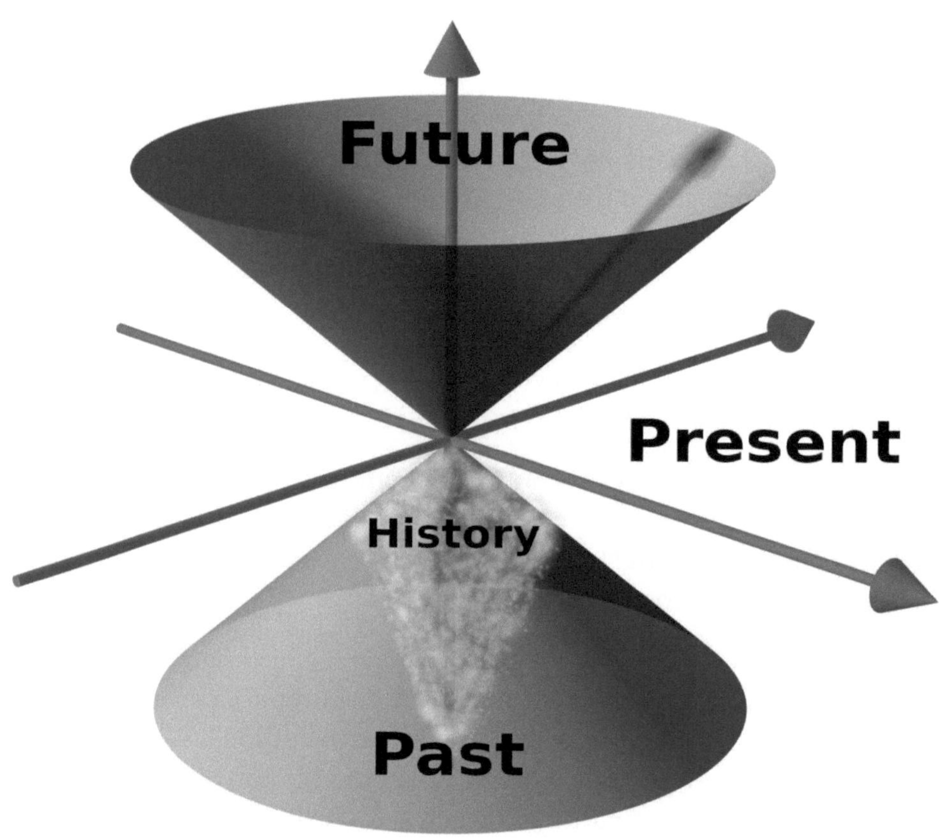

Fig. 6: Model of time with present, future, past and history

History as a model of the past

However, the distinction between the past and history has not yet been generally accepted. E.g. the Egyptologist and cultural scientist Jan Assmann expressed himself thus:

"The past only comes into being by referring to it." [Assmann 2005, S. 31]

This is roughly equivalent to saying *"If no one is looking, then the moon is not there."*

Eugen Gabowitsch (1938 - 2009), the well-known history analyst, criticised Assmann's statement as follows:

"Wrong! The past was, and when you refer to it, or believe that you refer to it, then you make a model, then you make history." [Gabowitsch 2008]

I continue quoting Gabowitsch [Gabowitsch 2008]:

"I call what happened in the past the past, and I call the fruits of the historian's writing - knowledge, representation, teaching - history. We know history well, it only takes time to read it.

History is a model of the past (also a system of such models). A model is everything, that is, a narrative, an attempt to represent something mathematically-statistically. Models are always only a very rough approximation of the object, in this case the past. History models the past, tries to describe it, to "reconstruct" it, to invent it.

The past cannot be false (only unknown or poorly known).

History can be false, bad, inaccurate, invented, mythical, legendary, etc."

Summary: Two main problems in the history of Old Europe and their solution

Solution:

The Bible's view of the creation of the world
has not been refuted by proving
that the biblical text is a forgery.

Better:

A more rational way of knowledge discovery
has been found.

->

Criticism of chronology and history
History Hacking

**Today's chronology of antiquity and the Middle Ages originated in a time with a different world view,
the geocentric world view including God,
superstition,
astrology,
number mysticism
and geometrically idealised representation.**

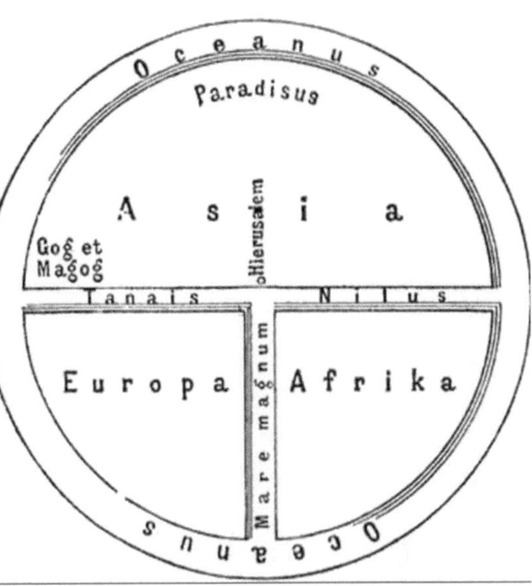

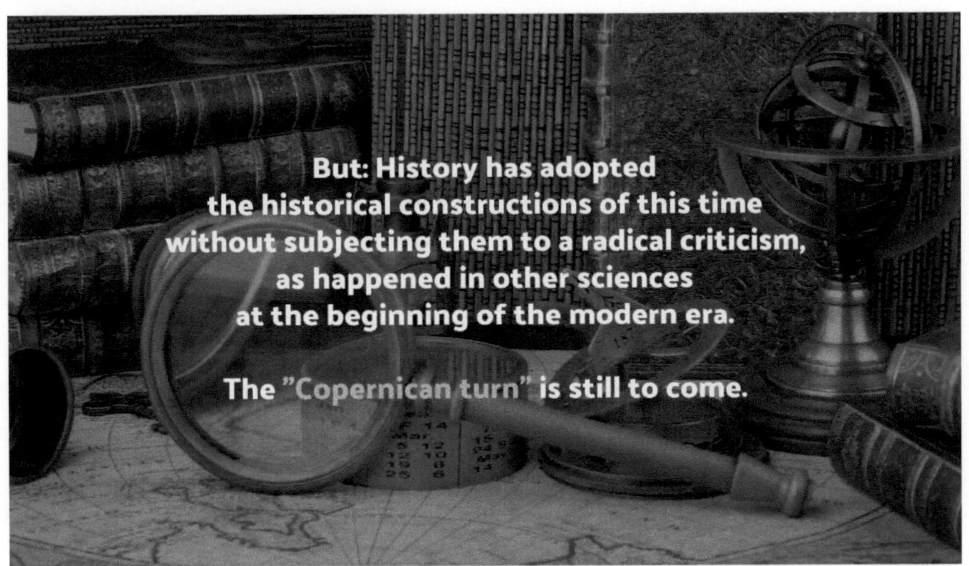

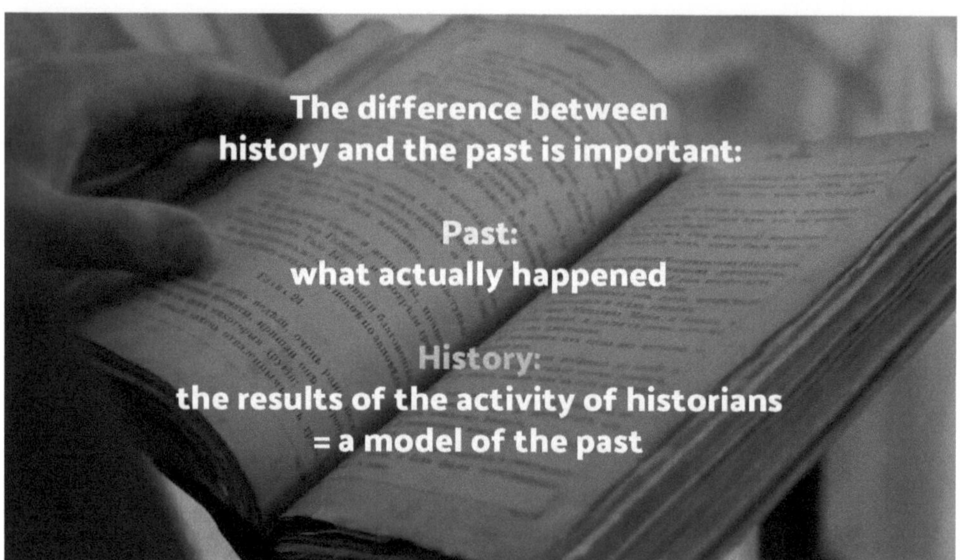

Anything goes

In order to initiate the paradigm shift of a scientific revolution (in the sense of the philosopher of science Thomas S. Kuhn), new methods of knowledge are sometimes required. This also includes methods of knowledge that already exist but are not used in all sciences. An extension of these methods to other fields of knowledge can then lead to completely new insights.

The philosopher of science Paul Feyerabend (1924-1994) holds the view that "anything goes" is the only possible description of the course of scientific research. In the sciences, the applicable rules have been violated again and again throughout history. It was precisely because of this that scientific progress was possible.

Fig. 12: Paul Feyerabend: Anything goes

Feyerabend brings up Galileo Galilei as an example, who adopted Nicolaus Copernicus' heliocentric world view, although according to empirical observations of the time it was less accurate than Claudius Ptolemy's geocentric system and thus "falsified" by Popper's standards.

By simply claiming that the earth moved without empirical proof, he was able to discover his laws of falling and thus refute Aristotle's theory of motion. However, hard facts and evidence were lacking - nevertheless, Galileo stuck to his theory, which could only be empirically confirmed ("proven") over 100 years later.

So it is not enough to argue within an old theory to overthrow it. One must not only be able to think outside the box, but also stick to it when there is resistance.

Only with "anything goes" can therefore be guaranteed that scientific progress will not be hindered. Then there can also be scientific revolutions, as the philosopher of science Thomas S. Kuhn (1922-1966) would say.

Fig. 13: Galileo facing the Roman Inquisition, painting by Cristiano Banti (1824-1904)

"Scientists solve problems not because they have a divining rod - methodology or a theory of rationality - but because they have been dealing with a problem for a long time, because they know the circumstances quite well, because they are not stupid (which is admittedly quite doubtful nowadays, when almost anyone can become a scientist).) [...]" [Feyerabend 1986, S. 388]

The development of new methods of knowledge (in the sense of Paul Feyerabend) leads to results that allow completely new insights into the history of Old Europe and have already initiated a paradigm shift.

Computational Thinking

In recent years, the approach of "computational thinking" has become popular in connection with its application beyond computer science. Computational thinking means something like "thinking like a computer scientist".

"Thinking like a computer scientist means more than being able to program a computer. It requires thinking at multiple levels of abstraction. [...] It represents a universally applicable attitude and skill set everyone, not just computer scientists, would be eager to learn and use. " [Wing 2006, S. 33/34]

The core of computational thinking is pattern recognition - as the basis for the associated development of algorithms. Pattern recognition serves to recognise generalisations and abstractions. With these algorithms, models of reality can then be created on the computer, for example, with which virtual experiments are possible without involving the real world (e.g. for animal experiments or the weather). The relevance of these models depends, of course, on the degree of correspondence with reality.

Computational Thinking thus includes logic, generalisation, abstraction, decomposition and modelling in addition to pattern recognition.

The historical-analytical approach of History Hacking pursued by Mario Arndt is primarily based on Computational Thinking.

The term "hacking", which is well known in computer science (but was already used among amateur radio operators in the 1950s), is understood here as an unconventional method of obtaining information that is not accessible using the current methods of historical scholarship.

What are the methods of History Hacking?

History Hacking - in addition to textual analysis in the humanities - makes particular use of methods known from mathematics, computer science and the natural sciences.

History Hacking includes *statistical methods,* the application of which to history made the mathematician Anatoly Fomenko famous ("History: Fiction or Science?"). According to Fomenko, these analyses show that the entire history of antiquity and the Middle Ages actually consists only of repetitions of the same few stories. According to Fomenko, the sequence of rulers and events of these millennia are only slightly modified duplicates of only a few actual stories. More on the research results of Mario Arndt: Hack #4, #5 and #6.

The *structural analysis* developed by Mario Arndt examines the sequence of rulers as well as other striking events to see if there are patterns and algorithms in them. This represents an application of computational thinking. Read more: Hack #1 and #8.

The application of *differential calculus* to data series reveals interesting inflection points in the curves of the derivatives when examining the values of historical variations in the Earth's rotation (the values of which come from the analysis of historical texts on solar and lunar eclipse reports). More: Hack #7.

By *analysing years and dates,* interesting connections between individual historical events, between the different calendar eras of antiquity, and between history and Holy Scripture (the Bible) are identified. Read more: Hack #2, #3 and #4.

Summary:
Four methods of History Hacking

Methods of History Hacking

1.) Statistics

e.g. correlation of the history of Old Testament Israel with the Carolingian Empire and the Holy Roman Empire

Israel	Carolingian Empire and Holy Roman Empire	Comments
1. King Saul	1. King Pippin	Ritually anointed as the first king of Israel / of the Carolingian dynasty in the Frankish Empire
Esbaal is king in the north for a short time	Carloman is king in the south for a short time	"Minor division" of the kingdom, which is only short-term and of no significance, after the death of the first king
2. King David (= Darling)	2. King Charlemagne (Carolus = Darling = David) he compared himself to David, but also to Josiah = Charles I of Anjou according to Fomenko	Great Warriors; Expansion of the empire and peak of power; Role models for later kings
3. King Solomon (= the Peaceful)	3. King Louis the Pious	Consolidation and legislation
Building of the Temple in Jerusalem	Building of the Palatine Chapel in Aachen	Construction of a symbolically important sacred building within approx. 7 years
Saul => Solomon: 1079 - 931 BC	Pippin => Louis: 751 - 840 (911) AD (Louis IV 900-911)	Pagan elements are still present; relapse into old customs; apostasy from the correct faith
Approx. 931 BC Division of the Empire Israel and Judah	843 AD Division of the Empire (911 AD final division) West and East Frankish Empire	After the death of the 3rd king, division of the Empire
931 BC – 597 BC	843 / 911 AD – 1309 AD	Period from the division of the Empire to the Babylonian Captivity
597 – 539 BC Babylonian Exile, also called Babylonian Captivity	1309 – 1377 AD Papal See in Avignon, also called Babylonian Captivity	Babylonian Captivity

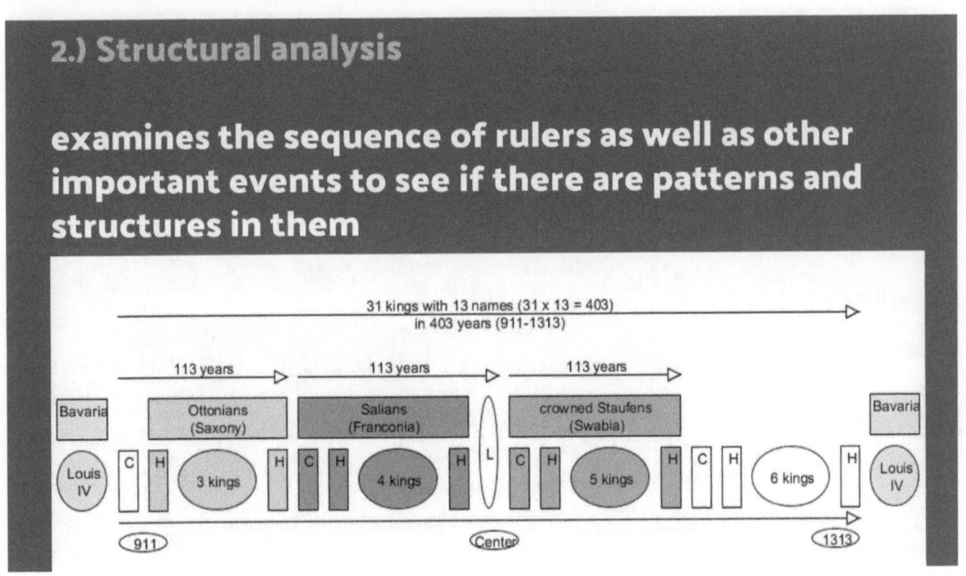

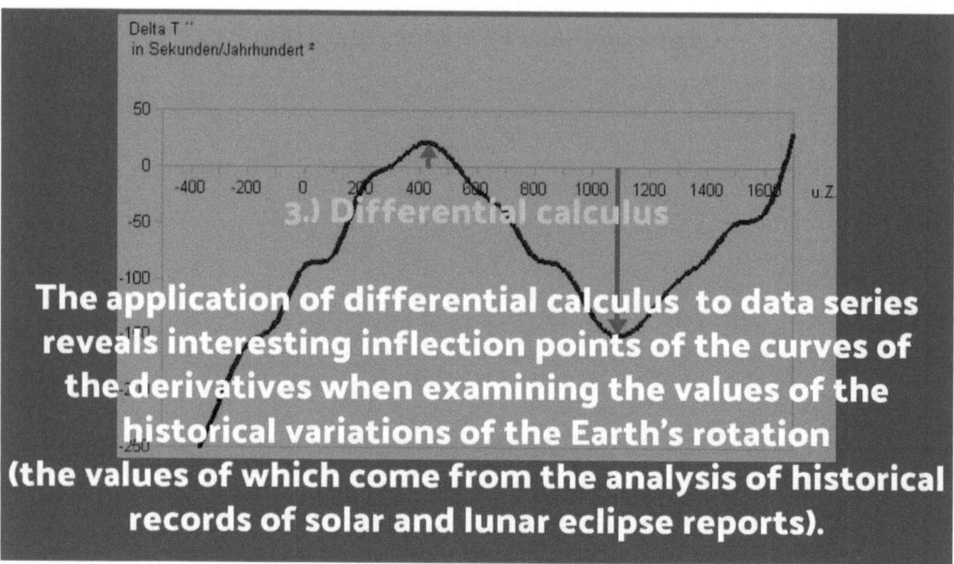
Delta T ''
in Sekunden/Jahrhundert ²
50
0
-50
-100
-250
-400
-200
0
200
400
600
800
1000
1200
1400
1600
u.Z.
3.) Differential calculus
The application of differential calculus to data series reveals interesting inflection points of the curves of the derivatives when examining the values of the historical variations of the Earth's rotation
(the values of which come from the analysis of historical records of solar and lunar eclipse reports).

4.) Analysis
of dates and year numbers

The structural analysis

Structural analysis is used to examine whether there are patterns and structures in the sequence of rulers as well as of other significant events.

A pattern is a scheme, a repeatable structure ("mathematics is the science of patterns" [Devlin 2003]).

A pattern sequence exists when objects are repeated according to a certain rule. A distinction is made between repeating patterns and growing patterns.

Pattern: a scheme, a repeatable structure.

**A pattern sequence exists
when objects are repeated according to a certain rule**

○△□○△□

Repeating pattern

CH1 CH1

Repeating pattern

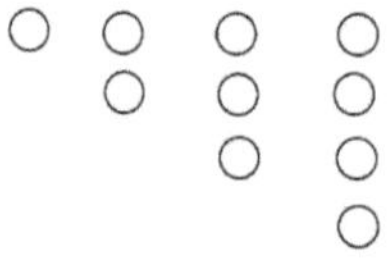

○ ○ ○ ○
○ ○ ○
○ ○
○

Growing pattern

1 2 3 4

Growing pattern

CH1H CH2H CH3H CH4H

Combination of repeating pattern sequence
CH[number]H CH[number]H CH[number]H CH[number]H
and
growing pattern sequence, number = 1 2 3 4

This is the pattern sequence of the kings of the
Holy Roman Empire from 911 - 1313.

C = King with the name Conrad
H = King with the name Henry

The analysis shows, for example, that the names of the Roman-German kings from 911 to 1313 are arranged according to the following combination of repeating pattern and growing pattern:

a. Conrad
b. Henry
c. List of arbitrary names of length x, where $x+1$ is the length of the following section, with $x_1=3$. So this is a recursive definition with $x_2=4$, $x_3=5$, $x_4=6$.
d. Henry

This pattern is repeated a total of four times in the time mentioned and can thus be described by an algorithm. Lothar III is placed exactly in the middle.

Fig. 20: "Roma", "Gallia", "Germania" and "Sclavinia" pay homage to Emperor Otto III

		Louis IV	
	911 919 936 961 983 1002	Conrad I Henry I **Otto I** **Otto II** **Otto III** Henry II	 **Emperor** **Emperor** **Emperor** **Emperor**
+ 113 (+/- 1) y.	1024 1028 1053 1077 1081 1087 1099	Conrad II Henry III **Henry IV** *Rudolf of Rheinfelden* *Hermann of Salm* **Conrad (III)** Henry V	**Emperor** **Emperor** **Emperor** **Emperor**
	1125	**Lothair III**	**Emperor**
+ 113 (+/- 1) y.	1138 1147 1152 1169 1198 1198 1212 1222	Conrad III. Henry (VI) **Frederick I** **HenryVI** **Philip of Swabia** **Otto IV** **Fredreick II** Henry (VII)	 **Emperor** **Emperor** **Emperor** **Emperor**
Thereafter (from William of Holland on all kings also crowned)	1237 1246 1248 1257 1257 1273 1292 1298 1308	Conrad IV *Henry Raspe* **William of Holland** **Richard of Cornwall** *Alfonso of Castile* **Rudolf I** **Adolf of Nassau** **Albert I** Henry VII	 **Emperor**
	1313		
	1314	Louis IV	

Table 1: The system of the names of the kings in the Holy Roman Empire 911-1314

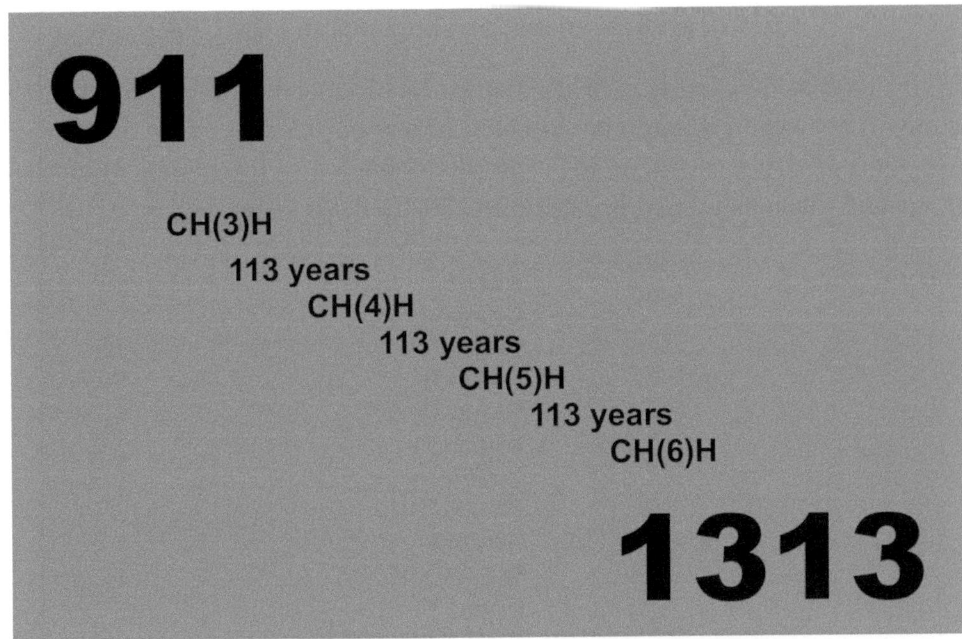

Fig. 21: The System of the Roman-German Kings from 911-1313

Result of the structural analysis: There is the same result in all the medieval Christian kingdoms of Europe that existed up until the Renaissance period. Until the 13th/14th century, the kings and other rulers are arranged in a fairly well-structured way. Until the 15th century, these structures continue in some countries, but become flawed. In Sweden, Russia and England this goes on into the 16th/17th century.

Objectively verifiable structures that can be understood by everyone are relevant for science. Especially when their existence is so improbable in a "natural" course of history, and they only occur in certain epochs. For example, these structures no longer exist at all in the succession of kings and other rulers in modern history from the 18th century onwards.

"Control groups" in modern England and the USA

If you look at modern lists of the names of successive rulers of a country, you will not expect them to be arranged in any particular pattern or to have any kind of structure. Here, for example, is the list of the names of all the kings and queens of Great Britain from 1707 to the present day:

1707	**Anne**
	George I
	George II
	George III
	George IV
	William IV
	Victoria
	Edward VII
	George V
	Edward VIII
	George VI
	Elisabeth II
	Charles III

Table 2: The Names of the Kings and Queens of Great Britain from 1707 to 2023

There is no structure here. The only regularity is that Edward and George follow twice one after the other. However, these alternating name repetitions can be explained quite simply on the basis of certain leading names of a dynasty and by deliberate choice of names and are therefore not the subject of this book.

From 1714 (George I) to the present day, Britain has been ruled continuously by the House of Hanover and, from Queen Victoria's son Edward VII onwards, by the House of Saxe-Coburg and Gotha (renamed "Windsor" during the First World War). George I was the founder of the dynasty, so that his name became dominant in the naming and is most frequently occurring.

The first appearance on Edward follows a deliberate choice of the royal name on accession. Edward VII's birth name was actually Albert Edward and in the family he was called "Bertie" (short for Albert).

The name Edward was already an important name in medieval English history until Edward VI (1547-1553). From 899 (Edward the Elder) to 1461 (Edward IV), every 7th king bears the name Edward (if the Norman period from 1066-1154 is considered a special case). This is described in detail from page 60.

As another example of the non-existent structuring of the names of rulers in the modern era, the presidents of the USA from 1789-2018 are listed below. Each name is listed only once, at the first inauguration. This rule also applies to all other lists of rulers used in the book.

There are some names of presidents that appear consistently from the 18th/19th to the 20th/21st centuries: George, John, James, William. The only conspicuous feature is that three other presidents reign between each of John I, II and III. Since there is nothing else conspicuous, this can be considered a coincidence in the total number of 45 presidents.

Start	End	Name
1789	1797	George I
1797	1801	John I
1801	1809	Thomas
1809	1817	James I
1817	1825	James II
1825	1829	John II
1829	1837	Andrew I
1837	1841	Martin
1841	1841	William I
1841	1845	John III
1845	1849	James III
1849	1850	Zachary
1850	1853	Millard

Start	End	Name
1853	1857	Franklin I
1857	1861	James IV
1861	1865	Abraham
1865	1865	Andrew II
1869	1877	Ulysses
1877	1881	Rutherford
1881	1881	James V
1881	1885	Chester
1885 1893	1889 1897	Grover
1889	1893	Benjamin
1897	1901	William II
1901	1909	Theodore
1909	1913	William III
1913	1921	Woodrow
1921	1923	Warren
1923	1929	Calvin
1929	1933	Herbert
1933	1945	Franklin II
1945	1953	Harry
1953	1961	Dwight
1961	1963	John IV
1963	1969	Lyndon
1969	1974	Richard
1974	1977	Gerald
1977	1981	James VI
1981	1989	Ronald
1989	1993	George II
1993	2001	William IV
2001	2009	George III
2009	2017	Barack
2017	2021	Donald
2021		Joseph

Table 3: List of US Presidents from 1789-2023

This absence of structure in the succession of names, except easily explained by leading names and deliberate naming, is hardly surprising and is in line with the prevailing opinion in historiography, which does not assume regularities or a planned sequence in the history of one or more countries.

We are therefore very surprised when we analyse the lists of the rulers of the Middle Ages. Here, in all the empires of Europe that existed up until the Renaissance period, including the Byzantine Empire (Emperor of Constantinople), we will recognise structures according to which the sequence of names is arranged, and whose beginning and end are clearly demarcated in a historically explicable way.

The "Roman Empire" from 911 - 1313

Back to the Holy Roman Empire!

There is a second structuring besides the name structure, a subdivision of the period from 911 to 1250 (339 years) into three sections of equal length, each with 113 years (+/- 1), each comprising the crowned kings of this period. These three sections each begin with a King Conrad, who is followed by kings with names according to the pattern described and whose last crowned king is followed by a King Conrad of the following section. The only thing that needs to be taken into account here is that Lothar III is placed exactly in the middle of the name system and therefore still comes after Henry V.

Concerning the possible deviation of one year, one needs to know that in the Middle Ages the beginning of the year was not uniformly regulated. In addition to 1 January, also the 25th of December, the 25th of March as well as Easter were very common. In the time of Frederick II, for example, 25 March was usually used as the beginning of the year in the Imperial Chancellery.

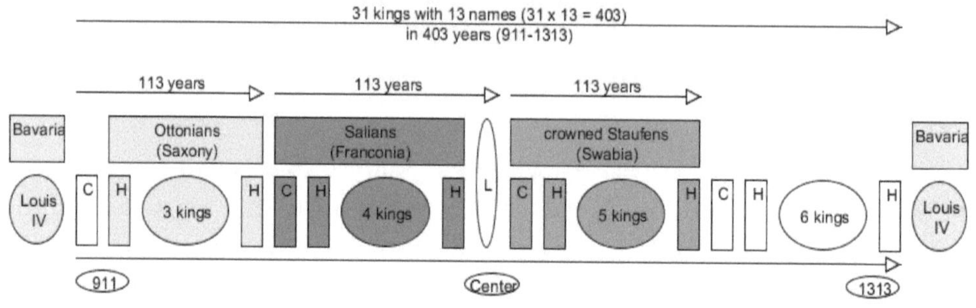

Fig. 22: The System of Roman-German royal names from 911-1313

If we now set a uniform start of the year on 25 March for the calculation, the exact 113-year grid fits. This is a second structuring that is superimposed on the name structure:

911: Conrad I
+ 113 years (6 kings)
1024: Conrad II
+ 113 years (7 kings + Lothair III)
1137: Conrad III
+ 113 years (8 kings)
1250: Conrad IV,
death of Frederick II

In 1250, Conrad IV was also king. According to the will of Frederick II, he was to take over the reign of the empire after his death.

The Eastern Frankish Empire and later Holy Roman Empire had five stem duchies in the Middle Ages: Saxony, Franconia, Swabia, Bavaria and Lorraine ("Empire of Lothar", also called the "Middle Empire"), of which the first four represent the major stems of Germany.

In the system of king's names from 911-1313, three of them appear: the Saxons, the Franks and the Swabians (Alemanni), each successively dominating one of the 113-year periods.

Lothair, as an exception, is placed exactly in the middle. And we find the Bavarians with the two kings from Bavaria Louis IV (same name and number) directly before 911 and directly after 1313.

The artificial character of this structure is underlined by the fact that both Conrad I and Conrad II, as well as Conrad III, were kings who replaced an old dynasty and thus helped a new dynasty to break through, which dominates the following period.

Conrad I was the first king after the Carolingians. He was himself a Frank, but through him the Saxon Ottonians came to power, who were then all kings of the entire first period up to Conrad II. According to the historian Widukind von Corvey ("Res gestae Saxonicae" I/XVI), the Ottonians already had de facto power in Conrad's time.

Conrad II at the beginning of the second section was the first king from the dynasty of the Salians, exactly 113 years after Conrad I. All the kings of the second period were Salians, with the exception of the two anti-kings.

Conrad III was then, again exactly 113 years after Conrad II, the first king from the Hohenstaufen dynasty, which dominated the third period, until Frederick II. Otto IV was the only king of this period who was not a Hohenstaufen.

Such an arrangement of the three dominant dynasties of the Roman-German High Middle Ages from 911-1250 in three 113-year periods, all beginning with a king with the same name Conrad, can only be explained by the fact that history here follows an ideal conception, a deliberate construction.

It is further interesting that neither the name Conrad nor the name Henry appear as East Frankish or Roman-German king names before 911 or after

1313 - exactly in contrast to the name Charles, where it is the other way round. So this is another pattern of the Roman-German Middle Ages from 911-1313.

Fig. 23: The imperial coronation of the last German king named Henry by three cardinals in 1312

So all in all there are four patterns that are perfectly coordinated:

1) the name pattern
   Conrad => Henry => x kings => Henry, which is repeated four times (as described above),
2) the pattern with the 113-year intervals between Conrad I, Conrad II, Conrad III and Conrad IV, whereby these Conrads also always correspond to the Conrads according to the name pattern,
3) the pattern with the arrangement of the three predominant dynasties (and thus the tribal duchies) into these 113-year periods between the Conrads,

4) the pattern of occurrence of the king's names Conrad and Henry (only between 911-1313) and Louis and Charles (only before and after 911-1313).

The "Roman Empire" from Charlemagne to Charles V.

Before and after 911-1313 there are no kings named Conrad or Henry. When analysing the times before and after, other names take over the function of the names conrad and Henry. These are the names Frederick, Louis and Charles.

Starting from the coronation of Charlemagne, 768, 357 years pass until Lothar III becomes king in 1125. He dies in 1137, 356 years before the death of the last king of the system, Frederick III in 1493. Thus, the only exception was placed exactly in the middle.

Before Charlemagne (768), the Frankish Empire was ruled by his father, Pepin the Short. Before that, Charles Martel had been the de facto political leader of the country as "dux et princeps Francorum" since 717. Charles Martel is considered the first Carolingian. After 1493 (death of Frederick III), the Holy Roman Empire was ruled by Maximilian I. The name Maximilian (the Greatest) is an antonym of Pepin the Short, who was king before 768.

Before Pippin reigned Charles Martel, the first Carolingian, and after Maximilian Charles V. It can therefore be assumed that the whole system was either designed during his reign (1520-1556) at the earliest, or at least expanded in essential parts.

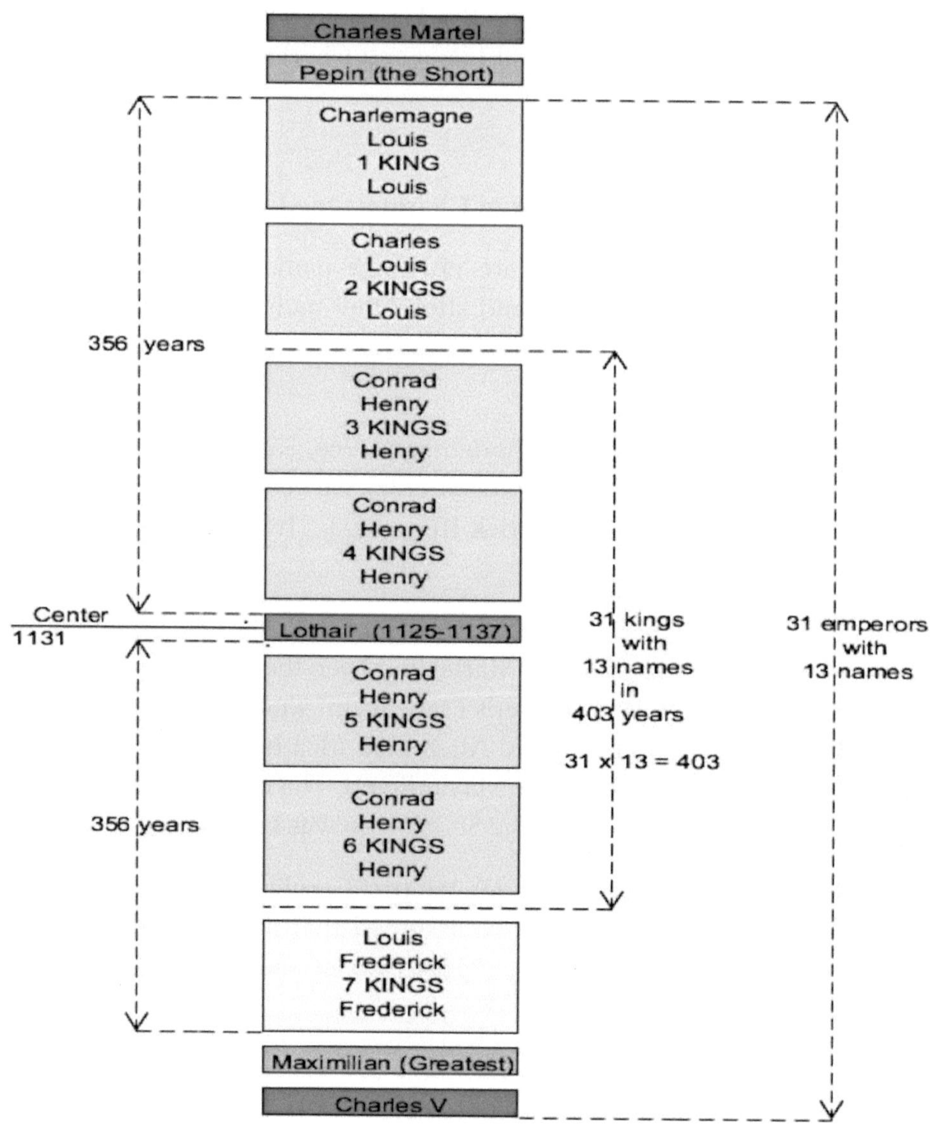

Fig. 24: The whole system from Charles Martel to Charles V.

Abstract description of the entire system from Ch. Martell to Charles V

The names of the rulers of the (entire) Frankish Empire and from 843 of the East Frankish Empire and later Holy Roman Empire are arranged from 768-1493 according to the following pattern:

a) X
b) Y
c) List of arbitrary names of length x, where x+1 is the length of the following section, with x1=1. So this is a recursive definition with x1=1, ..., x7=7.
d) Y

This pattern is repeated seven times during this time.

From 768 - 911 applies: X = Charles, Y = Louis.	**From 911 - 1313 applies: X = Conrad,Y= Henry.**	From 1314 - 1493 applies: X = Louis, Y= Frederick.

And this is what it looks like:

Charles Martel (First Carolingian) → Pepin (the Short)

XY(1)Y
XY(2)Y
XY(3)Y
XY(4)Y
XY(5)Y
XY(6)Y
XY(7)Y

Maximilian (the Greatest) → Charles V

Fig. 25: Jesus Christ hands over Philip II, also called "Dieudonné", to his parents from heaven, from the Grandes *Grandes Chroniques de France*.

The history of the kings of France in the High Middle Ages from 929 to 1322 can be divided into three periods of 131 years each (3 x 131 = 393 years). The structure of the French system is not quite as striking as that of the Roman-German system.

What in Germany is Louis IV, i.e. the name of the king who reigns immediately before and after the system, in France is obviously Charles, with the numbers III/IV. So the beginning is in 929, the year of the death of the last Charles before the system, of King Charles III, the Simple. The end is 393 years later, in 1322, the year in which the first King Charles after the system, Charles IV, begins his reign.

	Death of Charles III
Anno Domini 929	Rudolf of Burgundy Louis IV Lothair Louis V Hugh Capet Robert II Hugh Magnus Henry I
+ 131 years (A.D. 1060)	**Philip I** **Louis VI** **Philip** **Louis VII** **Philip II** **Louis VIII** **Louis IX** **Philip III** **Philip IV** **Louis X** (John I the Posthumous) **Philip V**
1322 (after 3 x 131 years)	Charles IV

Table 4: The system of French royal names 929-1322

An interesting fact is that the Carolingian Charles III is deposed exactly 6 years before his death, and the Capetian Charles IV becomes king exactly 6 years before his death. And as with the Roman-German kings, the first king who follows the system is also the last of his dynasty.

After Charles IV, from Philip VI onwards, the House of Valois, a side branch of the Capetians, succeeded to the French throne. Philip VI was the son of the founder of the dynasty, Charles I of Valois, and Margaret of Anjou, the granddaughter of Charles I of Anjou.

Within the 393 years, the last two periods of together 2 x 131 years starting in 1060 are clearly separated from the first 131-year period. In France, from 1060-1322, the kings have only the names Philip and Louis, taking turns of course. And if there are two Louis in succession, they are promptly followed by two Philips.

The only exception in 1316 was King John I, who was born after the death of his father and died a few days after his birth. The regency for him was led by Philip V.

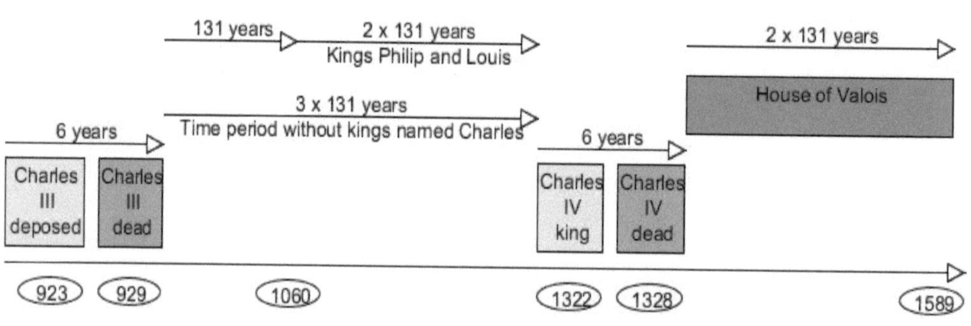

Fig. 26: The French system of royal names from 923-1589

In the last 2 x 131 years, there are Philip-Louis pairs with identical terms of office from 1059-1316:

- Philip I and Louis VII: 49 years
- Philip II and Louis IX: 44 years
- Philip IV and Louis VI: 29 years

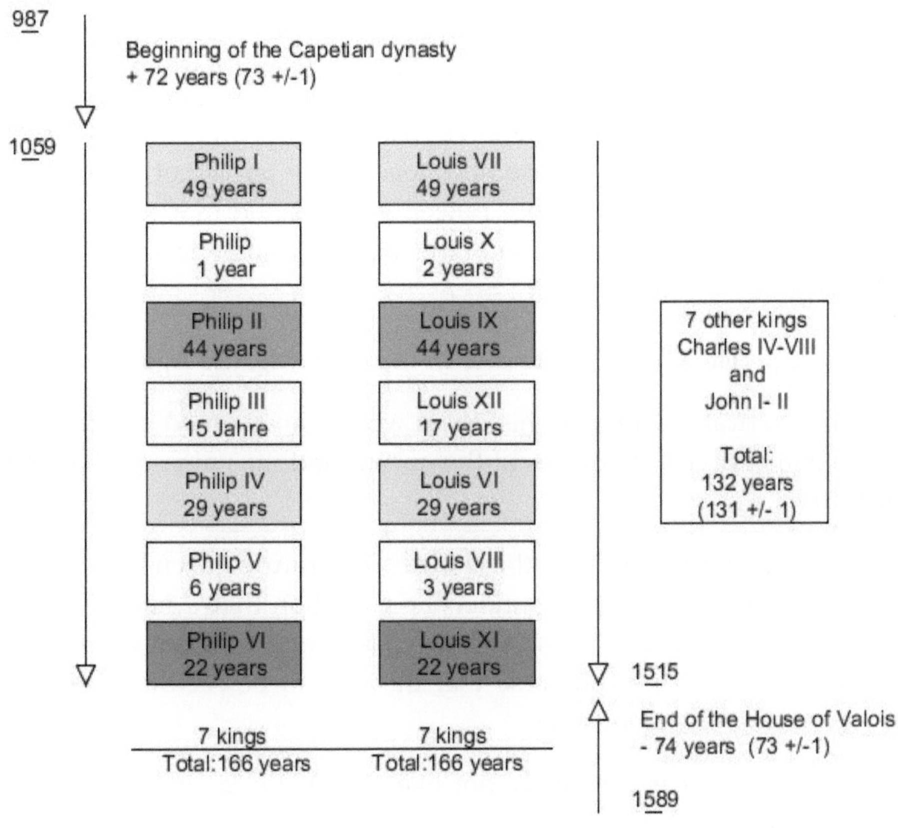

Fig. 27: Philip Louis pairs 1059-1515

Philip VI and Louis XI, who came afterwards, were also kings for the same period of time, namely 22 years each. If we add the time until 1515, when Louis XII dies without descendants and there are no kings named Philip and Louis after him for a long time, then we find the following astonishing fact:

There are a total of seven kings named Philip and Louis in each of these years between 1059-1515. All the kings named Philip and all the kings named Louis together were each king for a total of exactly 166 years, i.e. the same total length of time. During this period (from 1316) there are also kings with other names, seven of them (John I-II and Charles IV-VIII).

73 (+/- 1) years before, the Capetian dynasty begins, and 73 (+/- 1) years after that, the reign of the House of Valois, a side branch of the Capetians, ends and the Bourbons come to power. We will find more frequent intervals of 73 years in the structuring of the Merovingian period.

The Queens of France in the High Middle Ages

In a non-fabricated course of history, it would be assumed that there is no connection between the names of the queens and the names of the kings of a country.

According to written sources, the choice of the future queen by the king (or his parents) never took place under the condition that it had to be a lady with a certain name. Moreover, the dynastic and regional origins of the queens in France are so diverse that this cannot be seen as a reason for always having the same name.

This means that it is absolutely not likely (in plain language: impossible) that certain, few names of queens occur over a period of centuries exclusively with certain names of kings, but never with other names.

However, this is exactly the case for the names of the queens and kings of France in the period from 1060 to 1322.

The spouses of Philip I were called 1. Bertha and 2. Bertrada. Bertha is sometimes (according to official history "erroneously") also called Bertrada.

The wives from the first marriage of Philip II and Philip III were called Elisabeth (Isabelle). Elisabeth (Isabelle) is very similar to "Bertha" (today's Slavic short forms e.g. "Beta"). This then fits with Philip I.

The wives from the last (third or second) marriage of Philip II and Philip III were called Maria.

The wives from the first marriage of Philip IV, V and VI were called Joan, whereby only Philip VI (king from 1328, i.e. after 1322) subsequently married another woman named Blanche.

Blanche is the keyword for the kings Louis.

The wives of Louis VI's and Louis VII's last (second resp. third) marriage were called Adelheid.

Louis VIII's only wife was called Blanche.

The name of Louis VI's first wife, Lucia, is also identical to Blanche in meaning ("the shining one"). Blanc/blanche comes from the Germanic blank/blangkaz, meaning "shining" (according to official history via the late Latin blancus).

The women from Louis IX's, X's and XI's first marriage were called Margaret.

In summary: The queens named Bertha/ Bertrada/ Elisabeth, Maria and Joan have as spouses only kings named Philip. And the queens named Blanche/ Lucia, Adelheid and Margaret have as spouses only kings named Louis. Both three kings with the name Philip in succession and three kings with the name Ludwig in succession also have three queens with identical names, Joan and Margaret. Furthermore, all other queen names are also found exclusively with either kings named Philip or Louis.

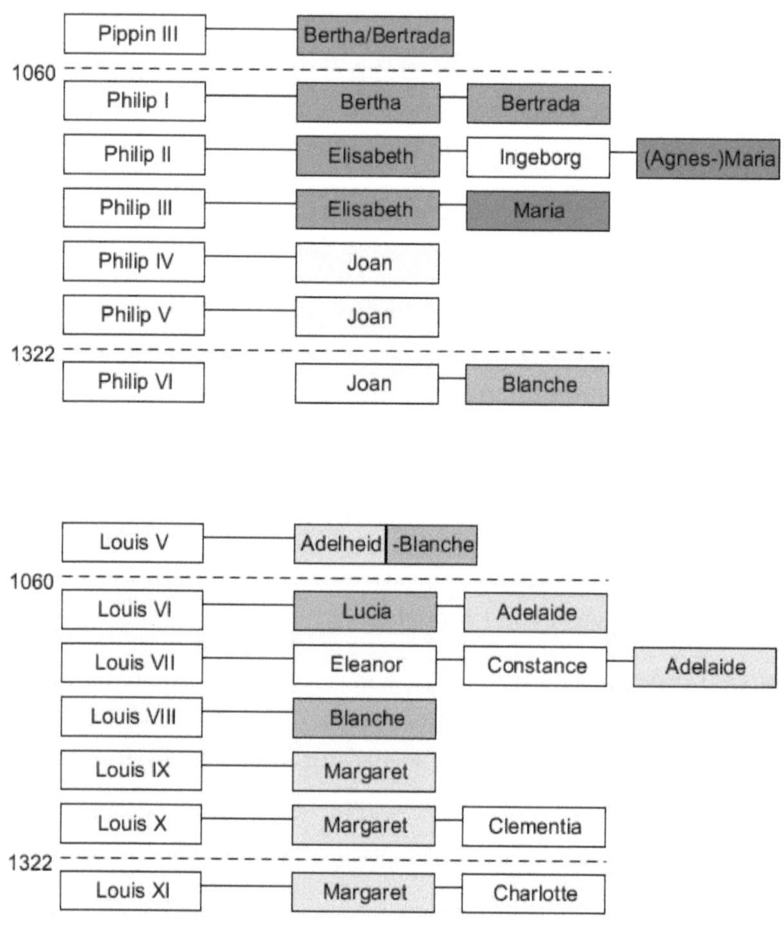

Fig. 28: The married kings and queens of France in the High Middle Ages in the 2 x 131 years from 1060-1322, arranged according to the two king's names of this period. Also listed here are Pippin (Pepin) III and Louis V, for reasons that follow from the text below.

Such a constellation is impossible in reality. In addition, this impossible constellation occurs precisely in the period 1060-1322, which is also characterised by the sequence of the only royal names Philip and Louis.

If we add Louis V (king 986/987, i.e. before 1060), we find that his only wife was called Adelheid-Blanche, which fits in perfectly with the other kings named Louis.

The parallels between Philip I (1052-1108) and Pippin (Pepin) III (714-768), the father of Charlemagne, are also fascinating, especially with regard to the wife(s). For Pippin III, the wives of Philip I were quite obviously copied, or vice versa.

In total, from 1060-1322, there are both nine queens for the kings Philip and nine queens for the kings Louis.

In addition: with the five married kings Philip and five married kings Louis between 1060-1322, there are also Philip-Ludwig pairs as with the tenures (follows next):

1 x married: two Kings Philip and two Kings Louis respectively,

2 x married: two Kings Philip and two Kings Louis respectively,

3 x married: one King Philip and one Kings Louis respectively.

Philip VI and Louis XI, who ruled after 1322, were also both married twice.

The names of the children are also drawn from a limited pool of names, so that repetitions are frequent.

By the way, these regularities do not exist with the kings named Charles (from the 14th century onwards). The later kings named Louis also no longer follow this pattern. As is usually to be expected, the queens of these kings have different names.

These are all absolutely impossible regularities that cannot be explained by coincidence. The creators of the official history have rather lovelessly copied together the queens of France. The arrangement of the kings also follows a clearly recognisable construction pattern.

Furthermore, according to official history, France is the only country in the universe to have managed, over a period of 328 years, to always have the oldest living son of the reigning king succeed him. This is the period from the founding of the Capetian dynasty in 988 (Robert II, the son of Hugh Capet) to 1316 (John I, the only one to fall out of the series of names). Other monarchies are already happy to create such a succession over two to three generations and a few decades.

This is therefore completely absurd and only an ideal of an absolutist monarchy, projected back as made-up history. The structure of the medieval system of royal names in Germany, on the other hand, follows the principle of federalism that characterises German history up until the present day.

The connection between the systems of royal names of Germany and France

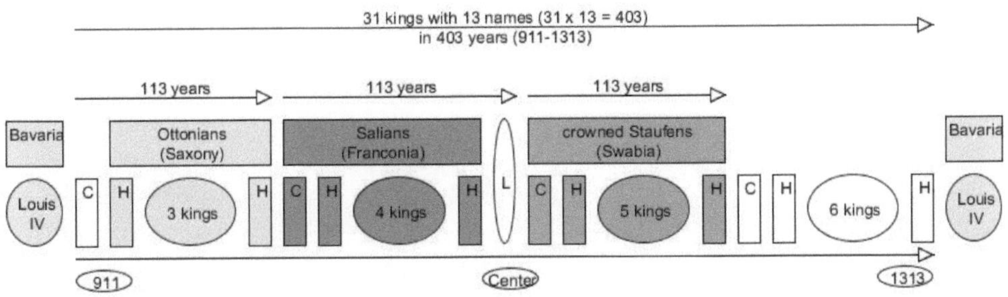

Fig. 29 (above): The system of Roman-German king names. C stands for the name Conrad, H for Henry and L for Lothair. The order of coronations applies, if there were none, that of election. In the Salian period, two kings out of the 4 in the middle are not Salians, and in the Hohenstaufen period, one king out of the 5 in the middle is not a Hohenstaufen. Note that in antiquity and in the Middle Ages the distances were not only formed with the differences usual today, but also according to the inclusive counting, in which the first year is also counted (also applies to France). From 1250 (end of the 3 x 113 years in the Holy Roman Empire) there are exactly 3 x 113 years until 1589, the end of the reign of the House of Valois in France.

Calculated backwards from the beginning in Germany and France 911-113 = 798 = 929-131.

The year 798 is therefore the common starting point of both systems. This shows that the two systems belong together, which is of course also obvious from the repeated occurrence of the emirp number 13/31.

Fig. 30 (below): The system of French royal names

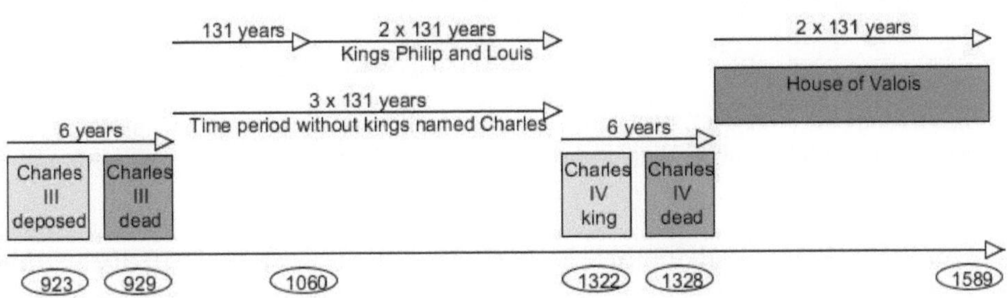

Fig. 31: King Henry VII (1457-1509) with his family (7 children), Saint George and the dragon. Prince Arthur stands behind the King on the left, behind him Prince Henry, later King Henry VIII.

The mathematician and history analyst Anatoly Fomenko (* 1945) has already shown that English history up to 1327 (violent death of King Edward II) resembles the history of the Byzantine Empire up to 1453. He is known for his statistical analyses of the texts on which official history is based.

According to Fomenko, these analyses reveal that the entire history of antiquity and the Middle Ages actually consists only of repetitions of the same few stories over and over again. According to Fomenko, the sequence of rulers and events of these millennia are only slightly modified duplicates of only a few actual stories.

However, the results of his research in this regard are not adopted here. Independently of this, however, the analysis of the king's names also brings further fascinating insights into the construction of official history in England.

The first king of the Angles (Rex Anglorum) was Offa of Mercia (774-796), although the sources here are not clear. He was the reformer of English coinage with the introduction of penny coins. The first king of the Anglo-Saxons (Anglorum Saxonum Rex) was Alfred the Great (871-899). The first king with the title "King of England" (Rex Angliae) was Henry II (1154-1189).

The conquest of England by the Normans under William I the Conqueror in 1066 marked a turning point for England. It ended the dominance of the Anglo-Saxon nobility. Linguistically, according to official history, the strong influence of the French language began here, as the Scandinavian ruling class of the Normans spoke French. The Anjou-Plantagenet dynasty that followed from 1154 onwards was then actually of French descent. The houses of Lancaster and York were their side lines. In 1485, the Welsh dynasty of Tudor came to the royal throne.

All regents are listed in the table only once, in the order in which they first took up their reign.

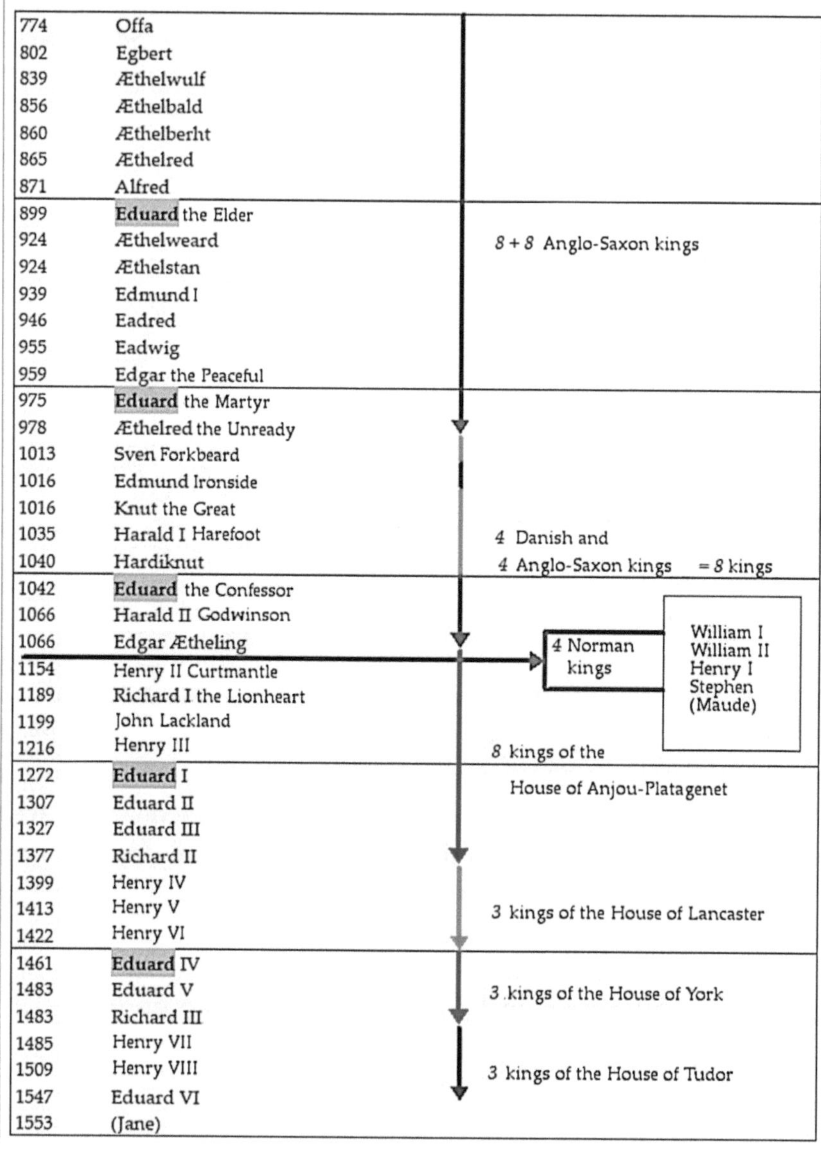

774	Offa	
802	Egbert	
839	Æthelwulf	
856	Æthelbald	
860	Æthelberht	
865	Æthelred	
871	Alfred	
899	**Eduard** the Elder	
924	Æthelweard	8 + 8 Anglo-Saxon kings
924	Æthelstan	
939	Edmund I	
946	Eadred	
955	Eadwig	
959	Edgar the Peaceful	
975	**Eduard** the Martyr	
978	Æthelred the Unready	
1013	Sven Forkbeard	
1016	Edmund Ironside	
1016	Knut the Great	
1035	Harald I Harefoot	4 Danish and
1040	Hardiknut	4 Anglo-Saxon kings = 8 kings
1042	**Eduard** the Confessor	
1066	Harald II Godwinson	William I William II
1066	Edgar Ætheling	4 Norman kings: Henry I
1154	Henry II Curtmantle	Stephen
1189	Richard I the Lionheart	(Maude)
1199	John Lackland	
1216	Henry III	8 kings of the
1272	**Eduard** I	House of Anjou-Platagenet
1307	Eduard II	
1327	Eduard III	
1377	Richard II	
1399	Henry IV	
1413	Henry V	3 kings of the House of Lancaster
1422	Henry VI	
1461	**Eduard** IV	
1483	Eduard V	3 kings of the House of York
1483	Richard III	
1485	Henry VII	
1509	Henry VIII	3 kings of the House of Tudor
1547	Eduard VI	
1553	(Jane)	

Table 5: The English Kings from 774-1553, 1066-1154 right (William I – Matilda), Eduard is also spelled "Edward"

If we cross out the period of the Norman dynasty from 1066-1154 (in Fomenko's analysis, this period corresponds to the occupation of Constantinople by the Crusaders and the exile of the Eastern Roman emperors in Nicaea), we see: From Edward the Elder (899-924) onwards, every 7th king has the name Edward, until Edward IV (1461-1483).

Two of the first two kings named Edward (Edward the Martyr and Edward the Confessor) were very religious rulers and are venerated as saints. For this reason, the dominance of this name is not surprising, as will also be shown in the lists of rulers of Northern and especially Eastern Europe in the following chapters.

The structuring of the royal dynasties is also striking. Of course, the choice of Offa of Mercia is not compelling at the beginning - but this does not change the subsequent clear structuring.

Until 1399, blocks of eight and four can be seen in the number of kings of the respective dynasties, e.g. 4 Danish kings and 4 Anglo-Saxon kings in the period after the first Danish king until the Norman conquest in 1066 - i.e. a total of 8. This is followed again by 4 kings until 1154 from the Norman dynasty.

If we put the important king Offa at the beginning, there are 2 x 8 kings until the first Danish king Sven Gabelbart in 1013, and 8 kings after 1154 from the Anjou-Plantagenet dynasty. From 1399, 3 kings each from the Lancaster, York and Tudor dynasties follow until 1553.

Further analysis of the king's names, the reigns and the dynasties reveals another system. Thus, the first two kings named Henry each have an identical reign of 35 years. Three of the four dynasties after 1154, after the Norman period, each begin with a King Henry. The successive kings named Henry from the House of Lancaster and from the House of Tudor also have an identical reign of 62 years. They are each followed by kings named Edward.

The sequence Henry => Edward => Richard of kings from the houses of Anjou-Plantagenet and Lancaster/ York is also striking. Thus, here too, there are regularities and patterns that should not exist in a normal course of history, such as in modern times.

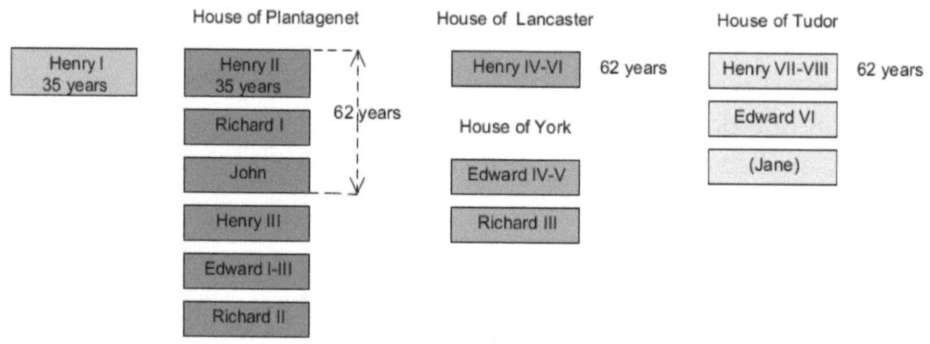

Fig. 32: The well-structured arrangement of the dynasties in another representation. You can see the Henrys at the beginning with identical reigns of 35 and 62 years respectively.

There is a striking little pattern of names in England from 1199-1553, framed by John/Jane, as in the Holy Roman Empire Louis and in France Charles frame the system.

1199	**John**
1216	**Henry** **3 x Edward** **Richard** **3 x Henry**
	2 x Edward **Richard** **2 x Henry** **Edward**
1553	**Jane**

Table 6: A "composition" of Henry (first, as well as three times and twice), Edward (last, as well as three times and twice) and Richard (each between the Edwards and the Henrys).

The period of the obvious fabrication of the king's names and the ruling dynasties is very close to the findings of Edwin Johnson (1842-1901). Johnson's research had shown that English history must have been forged up to the time of King Henry VIII (1491-1547).

He regarded the period from about 700-1400, almost the entire Middle Ages, as a later fabrication of Christian chroniclers and historians, filled with fictitious persons and events. According to Johnson, the writings attributed to this period (such as those of the historian Beda Venerabilis or Geoffrey Chaucer, the "father of English literature") were not written until the 16th century.

It was also not until the Tudor period that the name of the legendary king Arthur (also called Artus) was given in royal houses. This is very similar to the long absence of the name Charles after Charlemagne and the Carolingians in France and Germany and the late reappearance in the 13th century in France and in the 14th century in Germany.

In 1486, Arthur Tudor was born as the son of the first Tudor king Henry VII and and it was intended that he would ascend the English throne as Arthur II. He would have been the second Arthur after the legendary king who is said to have lived at the end of Roman times and at the beginning of Anglo-Saxon immigration, i.e. in the 5th century.

The city of Winchester was even chosen for Arthur's birth, which was identified as Camelot, the seat of the mythical king. However, Arthur died suddenly at the age of 15, so that his younger brother Henry later became king as Henry VIII.

In the Scottish royal house of Stuart, a Prince Arthur was also born as the son of King James IV in 1509, but he died the year after his birth. The son of the Scottish King James V, who also had the name Arthur, also died shortly after his birth in 1541.

Since several princes named Arthur, who were intended as heirs to the throne, died quite early, the name of the mythical king obviously could not establish itself in the royal dynasties, as happened, for example, with the name Charles in France and Germany.

As a result, other names of actual kings became more important in England and Scotland, and the name Arthur could never achieve the same dominance as the name Charles.

Russia and Ukraine

Fig. 33: The Russian national hero Alexander Nevsky (1220-1263) defeated the Crusaders and the Swedes, but became a vassal of the Mongol Khan Batu – according to official history.

In the official history of Rus and Russia, the names of the rulers (Grand Princes, from the 16th century called Tsars) are repeated in a well-structured manner. The entire history since the dynasty founder Rurik (862), and especially since the Christianisation by Vladimir I (980-1015) up to Peter I (1682-1725) is quite obviously constructed and made-up.

In the history of Rus and Russia, the centre of power has shifted since Grand Prince Vladimir I from Kiev to Vladimir-Suzdal to Moscow, illustrated by the change of the Grand Prince title from Kiev to Vladimir, and from Vladimir to Moscow. It is thus appropriate to analyse the succession of names of the Grand Princes and Tsars in this order.

The sections of Russian history defined in this way each begin with the first holder of a name and end with a further holder of that name, from 980-1328 with the second in each case. Between the first and the last holder of the name there are always exactly seven other grand princes or tsars. Here, too, all regents are listed only once, in the order in which they first took up their reign.

The first section (see Fig. 34) covers the two periods during which the Grand Princes of Kiev held supremacy in the territory of present-day Russia and eastern Ukraine. The first section of this (Vladimir I.-II.) is characterised by strong central power. In the second period, the Grand Duchy disintegrated.

The second part (see Fig. 34) begins with Andrei Bogoljubski, Prince of Vladimir-Susdal and Grand Duke of Kiev. Under him, the city of Vladimir became the centre of Kievan Rus, and the seat of the Grand Prince. Andrei Bogolyubsky also planned to move the seat of the Metropolitan (Head of the Orthodox Church Province) from Kiev to Vladimir. However, this met with opposition from the Patriarch of Constantinople.

The transfer of the metropolitan see also took place at the beginning of the Moscow section. At the end of the first section, Kievan Rus practically ends with its destruction by the Mongols in 1240. In the second section, the so-called Mongol rule over Rus and Russia is consolidated from the time of Alexander Nevsky, Prince of Novgorod from 1236.

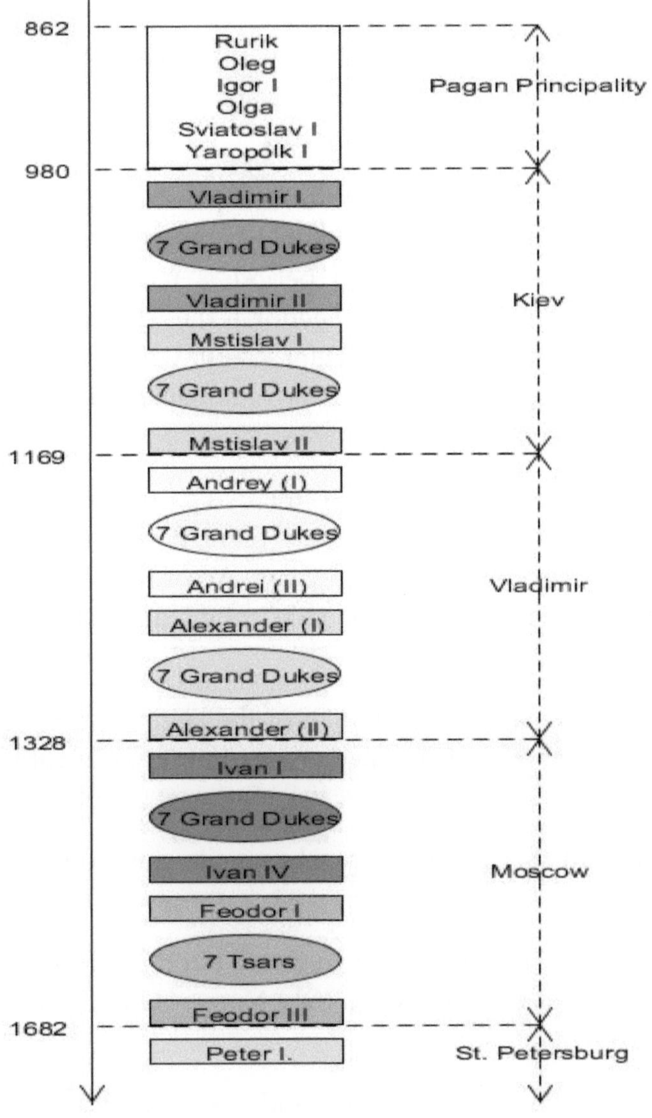

Fig. 34: The System of Names of the Grand Princes and Tsars of Rus and Russia in the 862 years following 862 AD

At the beginning of the third part(see Fig. 34), the shift of power from Vladimir to Moscow takes place with Ivan I, Prince of Moscow and Grand Prince of Vladimir. In addition to the Grand Prince, the Metropolitan also moved his seat from Vladimir to Moscow.

In the first period, there is a significant expansion of the territory of the Grand Duchy of Moscow, which was accompanied by victory over the Mongols and Tartars. The second period is marked by turmoil and a change of dynasty. It begins with Feodor I, the last Rurikid. In it the first Romanovs appear, the dynasty of Peter I, with whom it continues after the end of the Moscow period. The Romanovs remain on the Tsar's throne until 1917, the end of the monarchy in Russia.

The third part is practically as long as the two parts before it taken together. 1328-1682 cover 354 years, 980-1328 348 years. If Vladimir I came to power in 974, it would also be exactly 354 years. According to official history, he became Prince of Novgorod in 972, and Grand Duke of Kiev in 980 after the death of his brother Yaropolk.

A repetition can be seen in the names at the beginning. Before Vladimir I, Svyato-slav and Yaro-polk reigned. After him it is Svyato-polk and Yaro-slav.

The first name in this series, Svyatoslav, is also just a mixture of the previous names:

Rurik (Old Norse: Hrörekr), from German. Hrod- = glory/fame (and -ric = powerful, rich), and Oleg and Olga (Old Norse: Helgi), from German. helg- = holy, healthy.

The same meaning has слава (glory) and святой (holy), from which Svyatoslav is composed (Igor = Ingwar = protected by the highest god Yngwi).

With regard to the origin of the names of the grand princes and tsars, it is interesting to see that Greek names are practically only found in significant numbers from the 13th century onwards, although close relations with the Eastern Roman (Greek) Empire are said to have existed since the turn of the millennium, and also ecclesiastically the Metropolitan of Kiev (later Vladimir and Moscow) was subordinate to the Patriarch of Constantinople.

The only three exceptions before 1200 are Yuri (= George) Dolgoruki (1149-1157), the legendary founder of Moscow, and his sons Andrei Bogolyubsky and Mikhail.

From Alexander Nevsky (1252) onwards, almost all Russian grand princes and tsars have ("Slavicised") Greek names, with only three exceptions.

It is also noticeable that the numbers 862 for Rurik are repeated with 1682 for Peter I. And exactly 862 years pass from 862 (Rurik) to the death of Peter I, at the beginning of 1725!

Common features of the structures of the lists of rulers in Eastern and Northern Europe

Fig. 35: Stephen I of Hungary

Fig. 36: The baptism of Mieszko I of Poland

Fig. 37 (left): Cináed mac Ailpín (810-858), today also called Kenneth I. He was the first king of the Scots.

Fig. 38 (center): Gustav Eriksson Wasa (1496-1560) took Sweden out of the Kalmar Union with Denmark/Norway in 1523.

Fig. 39 (right): Queen Margarethe of Denmark (1353-1412). Her political goal was a great Scandinavian empire. Under her, Denmark and Norway were united from 1380 (until 1814). From 1388 she also ruled over Sweden - this unity lasted until 1523.

The systems of the names of the rulers of the other empires of Eastern and Northern Europe are analysed together. There is a very good reason for this, because they all show the same underlying pattern, which can be observed in pure form - without exceptions - in Russia.

The quite obviously constructed period in the later national empires of Eastern and Northern Europe (Russia, Hungary, Poland, Norway, Denmark, Sweden and Scotland) is characterised by uniform patterns whose common feature is the sequence of three to four blocks of equal length (Russia six blocks and Sweden irregular length), each beginning and ending with the same name.

In Hungary, Denmark and Scotland, the number of kings during this period is identical. In Poland and Norway (until 1204, the beginning of the civil war), there are also exactly 27 rulers, if the irregular kings are not counted. Again, Russia and Sweden are different.

The sequence of names of the Eastern and Northern European rulers of the Middle Ages in the periods described follows a similar structure. The well-structured Middle Ages begin in all countries, except Scotland, in the second half of the 10th century, in the context of the establishment of Christianity in the 10th/11th century. In Scotland it begins over 100 years earlier. It ends everywhere, except in Russia and Sweden, at the end of the 13th century or in the 14th century.

In Poland, Sweden and Russia, the reigns of Przemyslaw, Gustav Eriksson Wasa and Peter I were immediately followed by personalities who decisively reshaped the country. In Norway, the existence of an independent state ends with the union with Denmark. In the other countries, the well-structured Middle Ages are followed by anarchy, civil war and/or an interregnum, combined with a change of dynasty, immediately or a few years later.

In four of the seven countries, the first ruler over a country that can be described as "Christian" is preceded by six rulers over a pagan realm. In all seven countries there are then several blocks of equal length with several rulers whose first and last rulers have the same name. The length of the blocks is not the same everywhere.

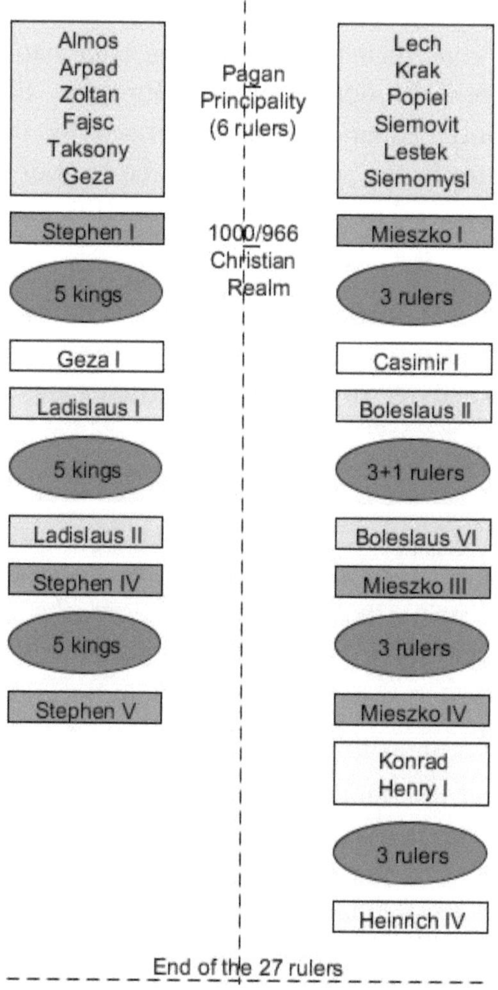

Fig. 40: Common features of the systems of rulers' names in Hungary and Poland (white: exceptions)

An interesting fact is that these structures only exist in Eastern and Northern Europe. The sequence of rulers' names in other parts of Europe is structured differently. These similarities reveal a common signature. There is no other explanation for this phenomenon than that either

a) all lists of rulers come from one source, or

b) a blueprint served as "guidance" for the preparation of the lists of regents of the other countries.

Another crucial design feature concerns the number of kings in the Well-Structured Middle Ages.

In three countries, Hungary, Denmark and Scotland, the number of kings during this period is identical. There are 27 in each country.

But in two other countries, Poland and Norway (until 1204), there are exactly 27 rulers, if the irregular kings are not counted. These are Zbigniew in Poland and Magnus and Olav in Norway.

The two remaining countries, Russia and Sweden, are also the only ones in Eastern and Northern Europe whose "well-structured Middle Ages" end after the 14th century.

In Russia and Sweden, the following common rule also applies:

Number of kings x number of different names
= end year of the well-structured Middle Ages - 2

1) Rus and Russia: 60 (grand) princes and tsars with 28 different names reign from 862-1682. 60 x 28 = 1680. That is exactly two years before the end in 1682 (Peter I).

2) Sweden: 49 kings/regents with 31 different names reign from 971-1521 (except for the three irregular Hakon VI, Albrecht and Margarethe I from 1362-1412, which is exactly 500 years). 49 x 31 = 1519. That is exactly two years before the end in 1521 (Gustav Eriksson Wasa).

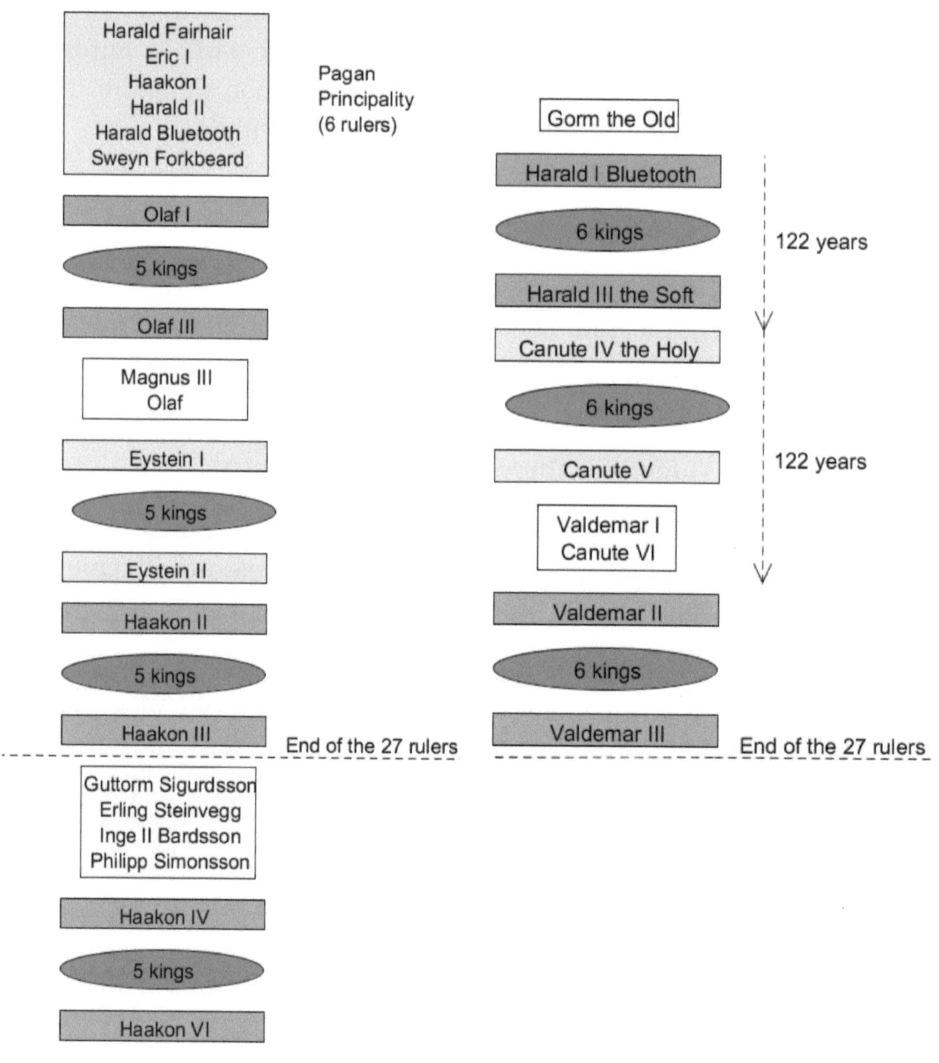

Fig. 41 (left): The System of names of the kings of Norway 870 - 1380 (white: exceptions)

Fig. 42 (right): The System of names of the kings of Denmark 936 – 1332 (white: exceptions)

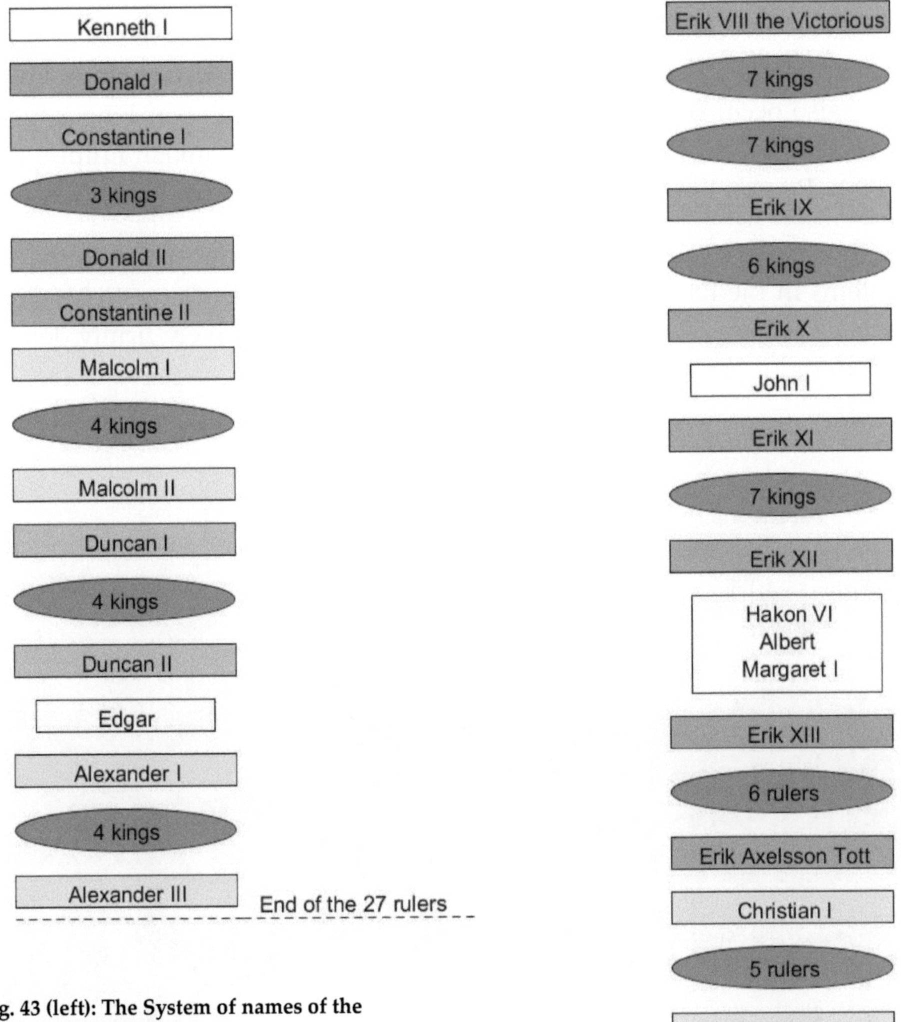

Fig. 43 (left): The System of names of the kings of Scotland 841 – 1286 (white: exceptions)

Fig. 44 (right): The System of names of the kings/ regents of Sweden 970 – 1521 (white: exceptions)

Regularities among the Kings of the Iberian Peninsula

Not surprisingly, absolutely unlikely regularities in the succession of king's names also occur on the Iberian Peninsula, in the predecessor kingdoms of Spain as well as in Portugal. Here the parallels to the Frankish Empire and the Holy Roman Empire are striking, as will be shown below.

First, however, let us look at the differences: The four most influential tribes/stems in the East Frankish and later Holy Roman Empire **successively** produce the kings for a unified empire, and this in relatively firmly delimited periods.

Fig. 45: The German and Spanish King and Emperor Charles V (1500-1558) with his wife Isabella of Portugal. He ruled over both Germany and the Iberian Peninsula. Is this the reason why there are striking parallels in the history of Germany and the Iberian Peninsula?

In Spain it is different: the four most important regions, Leon, Galicia, Castile and Aragon, exist in **parallel** in the Middle Ages, and are thus represented as separate states. Multiple divisions and (re)unions are structured via the royal names Ferdinand and Alfonso, as described below. Maybe there was a real event of this kind, which was then multiplied in the official history.

In Spain, there are names of important kings that were consistently given from the early Middle Ages (8th/9th century) until the modern era. This is a decisive difference to the Frankish Empire and the later France and Holy Roman Empire.

The transition from the Visigothic period to the kings of Asturias (the predecessor state of Spain) is analogous to the transition from the Merovingian to the Carolingian period ca. 717 - 741. Both in the Frankish Empire and in later Spain, the old and the new dynasties overlap - Merovingians and Carolingians as well as Visigoths and princes of Asturias.

The division of Asturias in 910 corresponds to the final division of the Frankish Empire (dynastic change with the first non-Carolingian in the Eastern Frankish Empire in 911).

Fig. 46: The Iberian peninsula in 1360

Also in both later Spain and the Holy Roman Empire there is the mark around 1250, i.e. 1252/57: Alfonso X becomes King of Castile and Roman-German (anti-)king.

And finally, in 1516 and 1519 respectively, the Habsburg Charles becomes King of Spain and Roman-German King and Emperor as Charles I and Charles V respectively. His wife is Isabella of Portugal.

Also striking on the Iberian Peninsula are:

1) Ferdinand is the king who unites: Castile/Leon/Galicia in 1037(-1157), again in 1230, and Castile/Aragon in 1479. Ferdinand I of Portugal (1367-1383) laid claim to the Castilian throne, therefore started a war with Castile but lost it - a failed union.
2) Alfonso I is the first recorded king of Asturias (the predecessor state of Spain) in 739. He conquered Galicia and Leon, and is considered the actual creator of the Kingdom of Asturias.

   Alfonso III and VII are respectively the first king before the partition (910 and 1157 respectively), and Alfonso VI and X is respectively the first king after the partition (1072 and 1252), after Kings Ferdinand.

   In Portugal, the namesake Alfonso I becomes the first king of Portugal in 1139.
3) Both Alfonso VI and X have a brother Sancho who also becomes king.

   In Portugal, Alfonso I and Alfonso II have sons named Sancho who also become kings.

Frankish Empire/Holy Roman Empire	Spain
- 717: The first Carolingian, Charles Martel, becomes mayor of the palace of the entire Frankish Empire, and thus practically the ruler. - In 741, Pippin the Short, later to become the first king of the Carolingians, succeeded him as mayor of the palace.	- 718: Pelayo founds the first Christian state "after" the fall of the Visigoth kingdom (721 death of the last king Ardo, 725 the last part of the kingdom, Septimania, was occupied by the Muslims). - In 739, Alfonso I, the first (confirmed) king of Asturias, begins his reign.
- In 911, Conrad I becomes the first non-Carolingian East Frankish king, after Louis IV, whose namesake Louis IV becomes king in 1313. This is the final division of the Frankish Empire. - In 922, Charles III the Simple was deposed as the last king of the West Franks (the next King Charles followed in 1322 with Charles IV).	- In 910, King Alfonso III dies and the Kingdom of Asturias is divided (Alfonso X is the first king after the "reunification"). - The biographical dates of the kings before the division, Alfonso III (848-910), and after the division, Alfonso X (1221-1284), are 373/374 years apart, i.e. there are 374 years from the death of Alfonso III in 910 to the death of Alfonso X in 1284. - almost identical ages: 62/63 years.
- 1250: End of the Hohenstaufen dynasty on the royal throne and beginning of the interregnum (end of the Roman-German sub-system of royal names after 339 years (911-1250)). - 1254: First mention of the name "Holy Roman Empire" in written sources. - 1257: Alfonso X becomes Roman-German (anti-)king.	- 1230 werden Kastilien, Leon (Asturien) und Galicien endgültig wiedervereinigt, - 1252 Alfonso X. ist der erste König danach
- 1519: Charles V becomes Roman-German King	- 1516: Charles I(V) becomes King of Spain.

Table 7: Correlations between the Frankish/Holy Roman Empire and Spain

Fig. 47: The Roman Emperor Constantius (250 - 306) appoints Constantine as his successor, not without heavenly assistance, of course.

In 324 AD, the Western Roman Emperor Constantine I defeated the Eastern Roman Emperor Licinius and thus became sole ruler of the Roman Empire. In the same year 324, he transferred the imperial capital from Nicomedia (today's Turkish Izmit) to Byzantium on the Bosporus, today's Istanbul. Rome in Italy had not served as a capital since Emperor Diocletian (284 - 305). Byzantium was renamed "Nova Roma" in 324 and has had the name Constantinople (Greek: Κωνσταντινούπολις) since 330. From the mid-fifth to the 13th century, Constantinople is the largest and richest city in Europe.

In historiography, the counting of the emperors of the Eastern Roman Empire, later known as the Byzantine Empire, usually begins with the year 324 and Constantine I. In terms of the status of the Roman Empire, the Byzantine Empire is identical to the Roman Empire from the first emperors onwards. Other decisive dates are the division of the empire in 395 and the end of the Western Roman Empire in 476.

During the occupation of Constantinople and most of the Eastern Roman Empire by the Crusaders, a so-called "Holy Roman Empire" first appears in the written sources in 1254. After 1453, i.e. after the fall of Constantinople and the end of the Eastern Roman Empire, there is then a "Sacrum Romanum Imperium <u>Nationis Germanicæ</u>" in the written sources, i.e. with the addition of the "German Nation".

Then, in the 16th/17th century, the Roman Empire is renamed the "Byzantine Empire" from Late Antiquity onwards. The inhabitants had called their empire the Roman Empire or Romania and themselves Romans (Greek: Ῥωμαῖοι). The Greeks used this designation for themselves until the Ottoman period.

At the same time, the history of the "Holy Roman Empire of the German Nation" was extended back to the Ottonians (911 or 919). However, it is said to have started in 962 at the latest with the coronation of Otto I as emperor in Rome, which curiously enough was still unknown even to Otto's court historian Widukind von Corvey.

There are even attempts to extend the beginning of German history back to a so-called Roman emperor "Charlemagne". He is said to have been crowned emperor by the Pope 800 years exactly to the day after the birth of Jesus Christ.

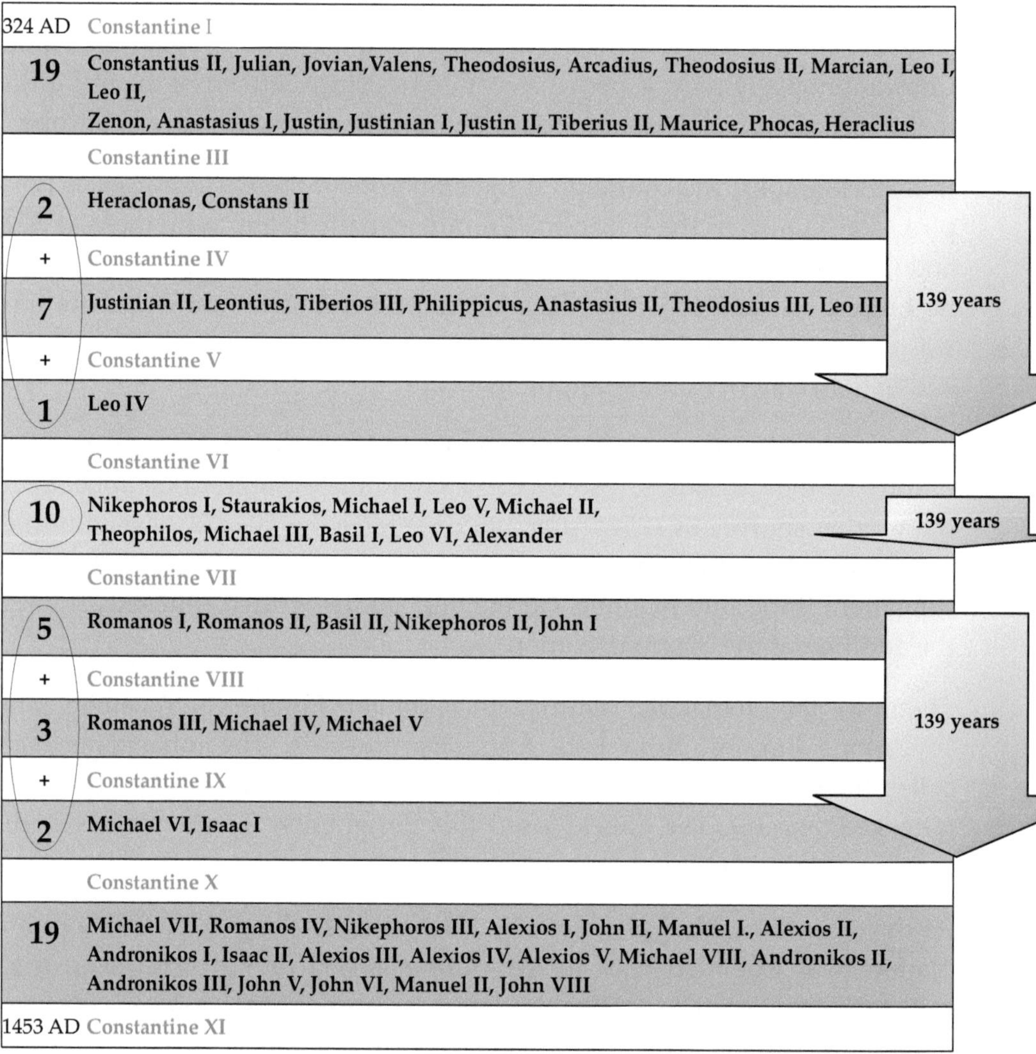

	Emperors	
324 AD	Constantine I	
19	Constantius II, Julian, Jovian,Valens, Theodosius, Arcadius, Theodosius II, Marcian, Leo I, Leo II, Zenon, Anastasius I, Justin, Justinian I, Justin II, Tiberius II, Maurice, Phocas, Heraclius	
	Constantine III	
2	Heraclonas, Constans II	
+	Constantine IV	
7	Justinian II, Leontius, Tiberios III, Philippicus, Anastasius II, Theodosius III, Leo III	139 years
+	Constantine V	
1	Leo IV	
	Constantine VI	
10	Nikephoros I, Staurakios, Michael I, Leo V, Michael II, Theophilos, Michael III, Basil I, Leo VI, Alexander	139 years
	Constantine VII	
5	Romanos I, Romanos II, Basil II, Nikephoros II, John I	
+	Constantine VIII	
3	Romanos III, Michael IV, Michael V	139 years
+	Constantine IX	
2	Michael VI, Isaac I	
	Constantine X	
19	Michael VII, Romanos IV, Nikephoros III, Alexios I, John II, Manuel I., Alexios II, Andronikos I, Isaac II, Alexios III, Alexios IV, Alexios V, Michael VIII, Andronikos II, Andronikos III, John V, John VI, Manuel II, John VIII	
1453 AD	Constantine XI	

Table 8: The Emperors of Constantinople from 324 - 1453

The sequence of names of the 78 legitimate ruling emperors of the Byzantine Empire, the Emperors of Constantinople (324 - 1453, Constantine I - Constantine XI), is well-structured around the name Constantine. The emperors of Nicaea during the Crusader occupation of Constantinople from 1204-1261 are not covered (analogous to England 1066-1154).

Both immediately after the first Emperor Constantine and before the last Emperor Constantine, there reigned 19 emperors each with different names. Between each of the total of 10 Constantines there are the following number of emperors with other names, each in the middle of the table (Constantine II was a Western Roman emperor):

324 AD		Constantine I	
		19	
641 AD	**139 years**	**2** **7** **1**	**10 emperors**
780 AD	**139 years**	**10**	**10 emperors**
919 AD	**139 years**	**5** **3** **2**	**10 emperors**
1059 AD		**19**	
1453 AD		Constantine XI	

Table 9: The Pattern of the Emperors of Constantinople from 324 - 1453

There are three groups of 10 emperors, each with a different name than Constantine:

2 + 7 + 1 = 10, in the centre 10, and 5 + 3 + 2 = 10.

With the adjacent emperors Constantine, that's a total of 38 emperors, the same as 19 + 19, the number of emperors before and after. It's all very regularly structured. Add to that Constantine I at the beginning, and Constantine XI at the end, for a total of 78 emperors. (With the second Constantine in the west, there would be 79 emperors).

The three groups of ten in the middle each last the same period of time. This, together with the other features, makes it almost certain that the list of emperors could not have come about in a "natural" way.

1) 2+7+1 = 10 emperors:

641 (Heraclonas) => 780 (death of Leo IV): 139 years

2) 5+3+2 = 10 emperors:

919 (Romanos I) => 1059 (death of Isaac I): 139 years

The period in between also has the same length of 139 years:

3) 10 emperors:

780 (after Leo IV) => 919 (Takeover of power by Romanos I): 139 years

The emperors with names other than Constantine are thus grouped as follows:

19 + (10 + 10 + 10) + 19

And all 78 emperors (i.e. including the 10 Constantines) are then grouped like this:

1 + 19 + (19 + 19) + 19 + 1

The system can also be written like this:

21 + (12 + 12 + 12) + 21 = 78

Everything fits together miraculously

Fig. 48: Joseph Justus Scaliger (1540 - 1609), the founder of scientific chronology. He was ordered by Pope Gregory XIII, who also introduced the Gregorian calendar, to create a coherent chronology that primarily covered the histories of the Greeks, Romans, Hebrews, Babylonians, Assyrians and Persians. However, Scaliger only became really well known after Jacob Bernays wrote a biography of him in 1855.

The result of the analysis of the ancient calendar eras will be the discovery of a clear plan for the construction of the individual calendar eras of official history. It is thus impossible that the calendar eras used in allegedly ancient and medieval texts actually have their beginning in the year that official history attributes to them. Either these calendar eras actually begin in a completely different year or these texts are forgeries.

In chronology, an era is a count of years starting from a specific point in time. An epoch is the beginning of an era. The epoch of our calendar era is the birth of Jesus Christ (this topic will be discussed in more detail in Hack #8). I will briefly list all the eras relevant for Europe with their epochs.

5508 BC - Byzantine era (Creation of the world on 1 September),
3761 BC - Jewish Era (creation of the world on 6 October),
753 BC - Founding of the city (Rome),
776 BC - Olympic Era (Greek count since the first Olympiad),
311 BC - Seleucid era (Seleucus I becomes king),
285 - Diocletian era (takeover of power by Emperor Diocletian), and
622 - Hejira (Islamic calendar).

So we have seven pre-modern eras. We add the beginning years of all except the Byzantine era to the left, the Byzantine era to the right, and we get:

776 + 753 + 622 + 311 + 285 + 3761 - 1000 = 5508

So the starting year of the Byzantine Era (creation of the world) plus 1000 years corresponds exactly to the sum of the other six eras.

Fascinating! (Mister Spock would now say.)

There is another era that Claudius Ptolemy invented for scientific purposes in the second century. This is the so-called Nabonasser era, beginning in 747 BC, which counts the years since the Babylonian king Nabonasser came to power. However, this chronology was never used by the Babylonians.

And even more fascinating: The Nabonasser era is simply calculated by subtracting the beginnings of the Byzantine and Jewish eras (the two world beginnings) from 1000:

5508 – 3761 – 1000 = 747

Of course, the Nabonasser era also fits perfectly with the other eras already mentioned. One simply has to subtract 2000 from their sum.

776 + 753 + 622 + 311 + 285 - 2000 = 747

A striking coincidence - the Jewish calendar

The year 1529 in the Christian calendar (Julian calendar beginning in year 1 and year change on 1 January) corresponds to the year 5289/5290 (year change 3/4 September) in the Jewish calendar, which begins in 3761 BC.

1529 = 529 + 1000 and
5290 = 529 x 10

Is this a coincidence or is there a system behind it?

If you subtract the number 5290 from 1529, you get -3761. The Jewish calendar (creation of the world) begins on 6 October 3761 B.C., i.e. with a different start of the year than in the Christian calendar on 1 January, which may result in a deviation of one year.

1529 – 5290 = -3761
1000 + 529 – 10 x 529 = -3761

I.e., 1000 – 9 x 529 = -3761,

or written another way: 9 x 529 – 1000 = 3761

The absolute value of the beginning of the Jewish calendar is therefore simply a multiple of the number 529 minus 1000. Can the other common calendar eras of antiquity and the Middle Ages also be calculated with the number 529?

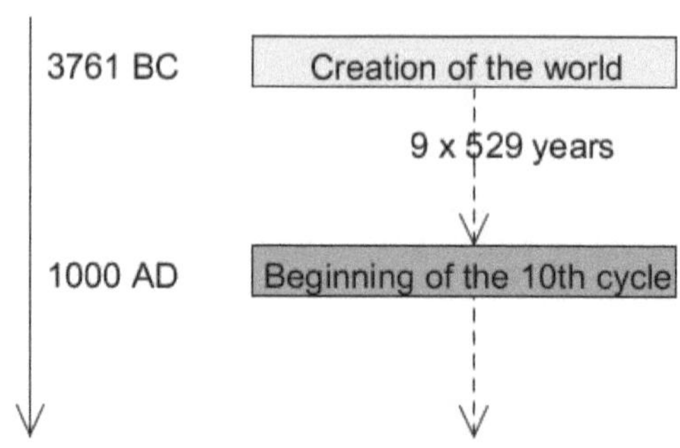

Fig. 49: Calculating the time of creation according to the Jewish calendar, starting from 1000 AD.

Equally striking - the Christian Byzantine calendar era

The absolute value of the beginning of the Byzantine era is similarly calculated with a multiple of the number 529:

11 x 529 – 311 = 5508

From eleven times the number 529 it is only necessary to subtract 311, the absolute value of the beginning of the era of the Babylonian king Seleucus.

One could also assume the following about the Byzantine calendar era:

311 – 11 x 529 = 5508 BC

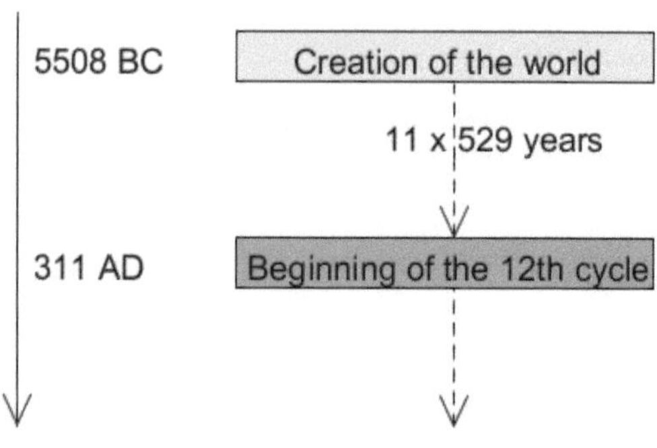

Fig. 50: The calculation of the time of creation according to the Byzantine calendar, starting from 311 AD.

It is interesting to note that we can easily convert the Jewish and Byzantine chronology into each other:

5508 = 3761 + 747 + 1000

Thus, the absolute value of the beginning of the Jewish era plus the absolute value of the beginning of the era of the Babylonian king Nabonasser plus 1000 equals the absolute value of the beginning of the Byzantine era.

The two Babylonian calendar eras and the two most important calendar eras of Greco-Roman antiquity

Since we have two calendar eras beginning with Babylonian kings (Nabonasser 747 BC and Seleucus 311 BC), it makes sense to look at this a little more in detail. And we can see:

311 + 747 = 1058 = 2 x 529

So the sum of the two Babylonian calendar eras is twice the number 529.

This makes us curious to examine the two beginnings of the most important calendar eras of Greco-Roman antiquity a little more in detail, 753 B.C. - foundation of the city (Rome), and 776 B.C. - Olympic era (Greek count since the first Olympiad).

753 + 776 = 1529 = 529 + 1000

This time it is 1 x 529 plus the number 1000, which gives the sum of the absolute values of the beginnings of both eras.

311 + 747 = 1058 = 2 x 529	753 + 776 = 1529 = 529 + 1000
311 = 2 x 529 - 747 747 = 2 x 529 - 311	753 = 529 + 1000 - 776 776 = 529 + 1000 - 753

Fig. 51: The Walls and Temple of Babylon

Fig. 52: Rome during the Republic period

The construction plan of the calendar eras

In summary, the construction plan of the calendar eras then looks like this:

11 x 529 - 311 = 5508	↑	Byzantine era
	+ 747 +1000	
9 x 529 - 1000 = 3761		Jewish era
2 x 529 = 311 + 747		Seleucid era and Era of Nabonassar
1 x 529 + 1000 = 776 + 753		Olympic era and era from the founding of Rome

The Diocletian era (285) is calculated from the figures already given, especially again the 529, as follows:

285 = 529 + 1000 – (4 x 311)

The Hejira, Islamic calendar, (622) is of course

622 = 311 + 311

This should prove that the starting years of these calendar eras could not have come about naturally, but rather at the scribe's desk according to a clear plan. This is probably connected with the Great Easter Cycle of 532 years (28 x 19).

The 529 in the chronology of the Roman and Byzantine Empires

In the following, some connections of the number 529 with the fabricated calendar eras of Roman antiquity (foundation of Rome in 753 BC) and Greek antiquity (beginning of the Olympiads in 776 BC) and important dates in the history of the Roman Empire are analysed. Interestingly, the analysis of periods with significant beginning and end years yields equations with exact century numbers (600, 700, etc.) as well as the 529th year.

Between the founding of the city of Rome in 753 BC and the end of the Western Roman Empire in 476 there are 1229 = 700 + 529 years.

So it is exactly 700 years plus the number 529, which is important for the construction of the calendar eras!

From the beginning of the Byzantine (Eastern Roman) Empire in 324 to the end of the Byzantine (Eastern Roman) Empire in 1453 (conquest by the Ottomans) there are 1129 = 600 + 529 years.

So again a perfect calculation with the 529!

Augustus, the first emperor of the Roman Empire

1229 years = 700 + 529

753 BC >---> 476 AD

Romulus, the first ruler of Rome

Romulus Augustus, the last ruler and emperor of the (Western) Roman Empire

Fig. 53: The construction number 529 in the history of the Roman Empire

Konstantin I,
the first emperor of the
Eastern Roman Empire
and of Constantinople

1129 years = 600 + 529

324 AD >---> 1453 AD

Konstantin XI,
the last emperor of the
Eastern Roman Empire
and of Constantinople

Fig. 54: The construction number 529 in the history of the Byzantine (Eastern Roman) Empire

From 776 BC to 1453 (conquest of Constantinople and thus the fall of the Eastern Roman Empire) 2229 years pass. That is 1000 years more than from the founding of Rome (753 BC) to the fall of the Western Roman Empire (476).

2229 = 1000 + 700 + 529

The beginning years also fit perfectly with the respective other end years and result in exact century figures:

324 + 476 = 800
1453 – 753 = 700

And with the founding of the city of Rome (753 BC), the fall of the Eastern Roman Empire (1453) and the number 529, the fall of the Western Roman Empire results like this:

1453 – 753 – 753 + 529 = 476

From 776 BC to the founding of Constantinople in 324, 275 Olympiads of 4 years each pass, i.e. 1100 = 600 + 500 years, again a perfect calculation!

The founding of Constantinople is therefore at the beginning of the 276th Olympiad. We may assume that the same final digits "76" at 776 BC (year count since the first Olympiad) and 476 (fall of the Western Roman Empire) are also not a coincidence.

The absolute values result in a difference of 300 years.

776 – 476 = 300

That everything fits together is already clear from the two dates at the beginning (753 BC foundation of Rome) and at the end (1453 fall of Eastern Rome). They both have a "53" in them and the amounts differ by 700.

I have summarised these connections in the following graphic:

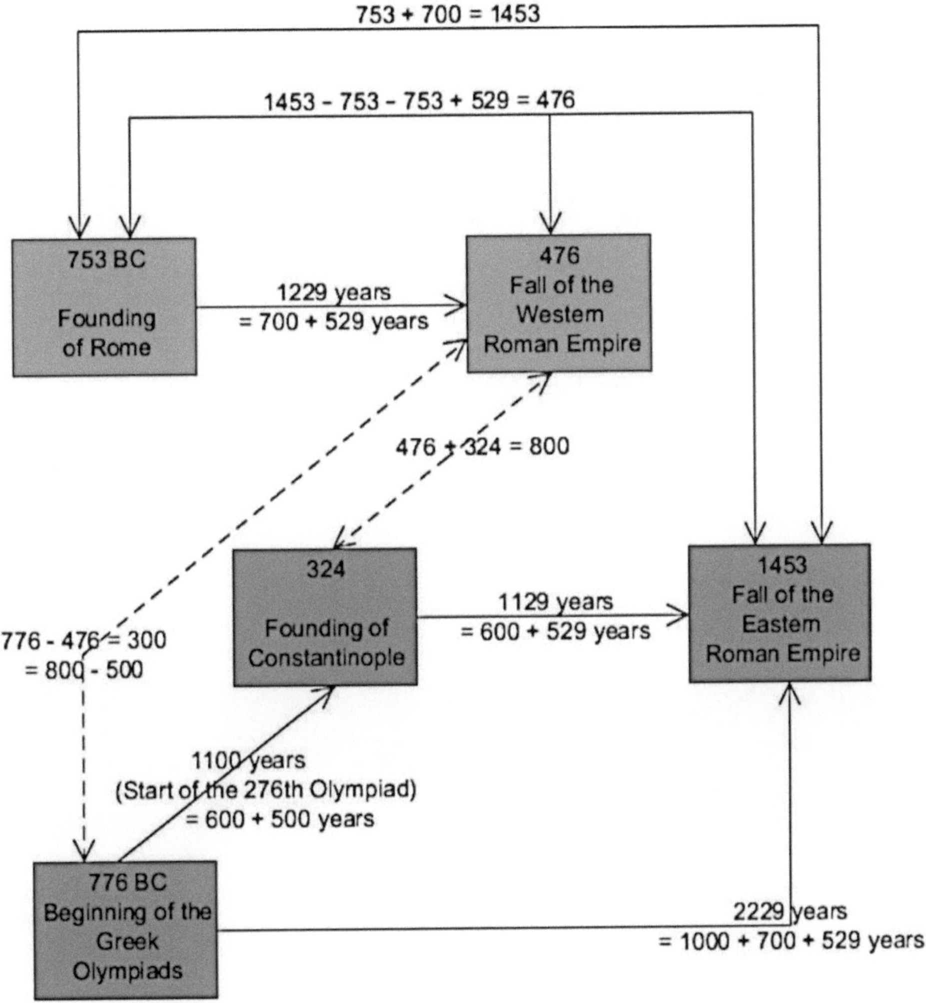

Fig. 55: The connection of the number 529 with the calendar eras of Greek and Roman antiquity and dates of the Roman Empire.

529

Introduction

Beginning with Ivan Panin (1855-1942), a number of authors have explored number patterns in the Hebrew text of the Old Testament and the Greek text of the New Testament. These patterns involve counting letters and words as well as discoveries made possible through the use of gematria.

Gematria is the assignment of numerical values to letters so that their relationships to each other can then be analysed. In both the Hebrew and Greek alphabets, letters are assigned certain numerical values based on their position in the alphabet, which can also be used to represent numbers. Each word can therefore also be read as a group of numbers. The sum of these individual numbers for the letters then results in the numerical value of a word.

Hack #3 is the author's discovery that this numerical code of the Bible also reappears in history, precisely in those places where, according to Hack #1, as a result of the structural analysis of the rulers' lists, absolutely unlikely anomalies exist, such as the 31 kings with 13 names in 403 years (31 x 13) from 911 - 1313 in the Holy Roman Empire.

"The Holographic Generating Set" 27 - 37 - 73

According to "The Bible Wheel" [McGough 2006], the numbers 27, 37 and 73 are the three numbers that form the basic framework of the numerical construction of the Bible. It is interesting to note that this is also true for the construction of the official history. It should be mentioned here that two other important pairs of numbers 13/31 and 14/41 result directly from the combination of 27, 37 and 73.

The starting point are the star numbers (1), 13, 37 and 73. A star number is a centred hexagram (six-pointed star), like the Star of David.

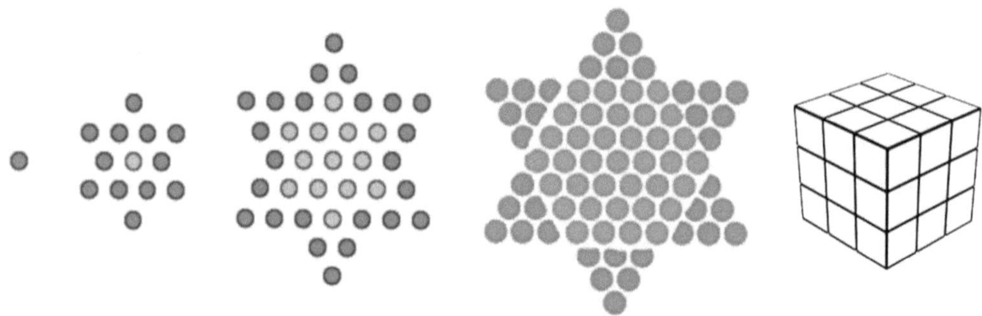

Fig.. 56: The star numbers 1, 13, 37 and 73 (with 37 as an enclosed hexagon) as well as the cube number 27 = 3 x 3 x 3

Fig. 57: Star of David: "The Star of David is interpreted as a symbolic representation of the relationship between man and God. The triangle pointing downwards says: Man has received his life from God. The triangle pointing upwards says: man will return to God. The twelve corners of the star are supposed to represent the Twelve Tribes of Israel. In addition, the six triangles represent the six days of creation and the large hexagon in the centre represents the seventh day, the day of rest." [wikipedia]

The numerical code of the Old Testament (Genesis 1:1) in history

Known for a long time: The numerical code of the Bible

The beginning of Genesis, chapter 1, results with numerical values of the Hebrew letters in **2701 = 37 x 73**

בראשית ברא אלהים את השמים ואת הארץ

In the beginning God created the heaven and the earth

913 + 203 + 86 + 401 + 395 + 407 + 296 = **2701**

2701 = 37 x 73 (2 Prime numbers)

This construction with the prime numbers 37 and 73 also exists in history, with the kings of the Merovingian dynasty in the Frankish Empire. The Merovingians are considered by both German and French history to be the first dynasty in their history. Clovis I becomes the first Christian Frankish king around 500 AD.

Clotar II becomes king 73 years after Chlotar I, and Chlotar III becomes king 73 years after Chlotar II and, on top of that, dies in a year ending in 73, in 673.

The kings Chlodwig (Clovis) I, Chlodwig (Clovis) II and Chlodwig (Clovis) III are aligned on the grid 2 x 73 + 37 years, with the years of the end of their reign (death), and the kings Childebert I, Childebert adoptivus and Childebert III, with the years of the beginning of their reign.

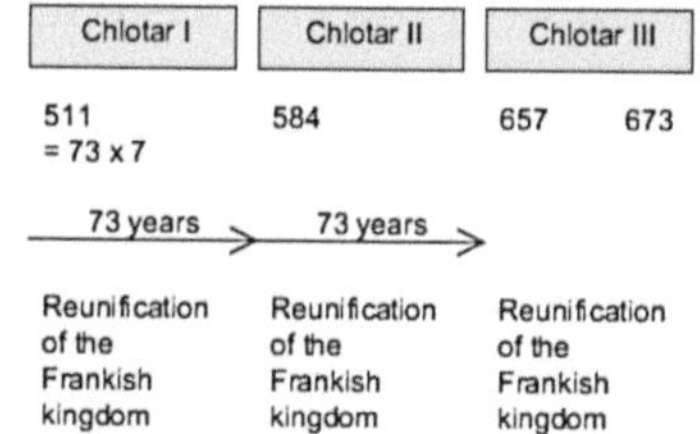

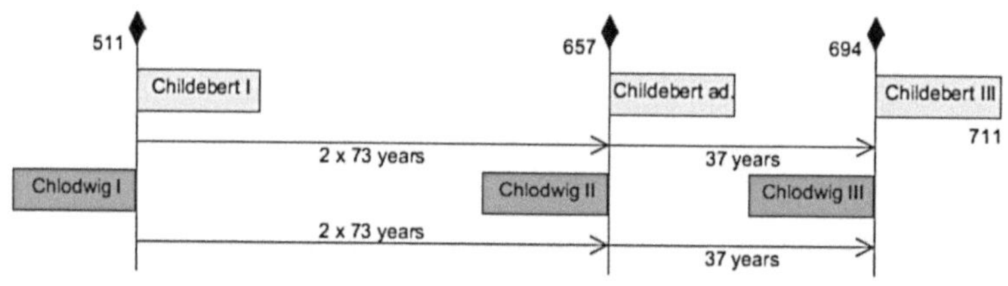

Fig. 58: The kings of the Merovingian dynasty in the grid 73 - 37 according to the pattern of Genesis 1,1

The numerical code of the New Testament (John 1:1) in history

Ἐν ἀρχῇ ἦν ὁ λόγος καὶ ὁ λόγος ἦν πρὸς τὸν θεόν καὶ θεὸς ἦν ὁ λόγος.

In the beginning was the Word, and the Word was with God, and the Word was God.

55 + 719 + 58 + 70 + 373 + 31 + 70 + 373 + 58 + 450 + 420 + 134 + 31 + 284 + 58 + 70 + 373 = 3627

3627 = 39 x 93 = 13 x 31 x 3 x 3

113 x 131 x 3 x 3 = 339 x 393

This construction of John 1:1 exists also in history,
in the systems of the names of the kings
of the Holy Roman Empire and France (Hack #1).

31 kings with 13 names in 13 x 31 years
3 x 113 = 339 years und 3 x 131 = 393 years

In the Holy Roman Empire there are 31 kings with 13 different names from 911 - 1313 (31 x 13 = 403 years). The period from 911 - 1250 lasts 3 x 113 = 339 years.

In France there are no kings named Charles from 929-1322 (3 x 131 = 393 years). From 1060 - 1322 (2 x 131 years) there are only kings named Philip or Louis.

King David and Successors

In the Gospel of Matthew, the number 14 appears in a chronological sense:

"On the whole, then, from Abraham to David there are fourteen generations, from David to the Babylonian Captivity fourteen generations, and from the Babylonian Captivity to Christ fourteen generations." (Matthew 1:17)

The number 14 now definitely refers to King David, who is also explicitly mentioned in the quoted text. Jesus Christ is also called the "new David". The numerical value of David (Hebrew: דוד) in the Hebrew alphabet is 14.

ד (Dalet) = 4, and ו (Vav) = 6

4 + 4 + 6 = 14

The construction numbers 27 and 73 are connected via the David number 14 and its mirror number 41.

14 + 27 = 41 and 41 + 73 = 114

Fig. 59: David with the head of Goliath, whom he had just defeated (painting by Caravaggio)

Such numerical values, which result from combinations of these numbers 14, 41, 27 and 73, exist in history as year numbers especially

1) in the first century B.C. and in the first century A.D. in the Roman Empire (Julian-Claudian dynasty and Flavians - historiographer Suetonius), as well as

2) from the 7th - 9th centuries in the Frankish Empire (dynasties of the Arnulfingers, Pippinids and Carolingians - historiography inspired by Suetonius' writings, especially in the case of Charlemagne).

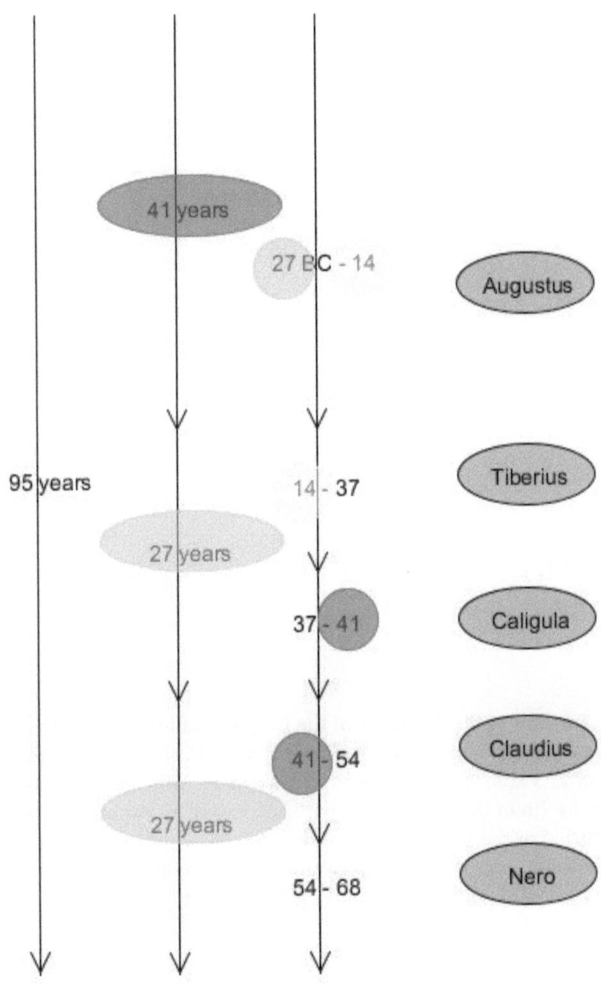

Fig. 60: The structuring of the time of the emperors of the Julian-Claudian dynasty in the Roman Empire. The life of Jesus Christ, also known as the "new David", falls in the time of the emperors Augustus and Tiberius.

Name	Born	Difference	Mayor of the Palace / King	Difference	Died
Pepin the Elder	580	ca. 43	623	17	640
Arnulf of Metz	582	ca. 32	614 (Bishop)	26	640
Grimoald the Elder	615	25	643	ca. 17	656-662
Pepin of Herstal	635-645 (640)	ca. 47	(679)/Total kingdom: 687	26	714
Charles Martel	688	26	714	27	741
Pepin the Short	714	27	741/ (742)	27	768
Charle-magne	742/ (747)	26	768	46	814
Louis the Pious	778	36	814	26	840

Table 10: The construction of the dynasties of the Pippinids and Carolingians in the Frankish Empire from 580 - 840. The concentration of numbers ending with 14 and 41 is immediately apparent, as well as time intervals of 27 years, sometimes even a year apart. This conspicuous feature is consistently documented from the 7th to the 9th century, with successive mayor of the palace or kings. This is similar to the structuring of the period from 100 BC - AD 96, which is also described in biographies of Suetonius. Charlemagne compared the Franks to the ancient Israelites and saw himself as the new David. He also had himself addressed at court as "new David".

9/11

On a 9th of 11 (Av) of the Jewish calendar, God punishes the people of Israel for their unbelief: *"I will fix for you this day as a day of crying ..."*

Known are the five calamities according to the Jewish Torah on the 9th of Av:

1. At the time of the Exodus from Egypt (1313 BC), the people of Israel were told in the desert that they would have to wander for 40 years.
2. The Temple of Jerusalem, built by Solomon, and the Kingdom of Judah are destroyed by the Babylonians in 586 BC - the Babylonian Captivity begins.
3. The Second Temple of Jerusalem is destroyed by the Romans in 70 AD.
4. The Bar Kochbar rebellion against the Romans is put down.
5. Jerusalem is razed to the ground by the Romans in 136 AD.

Germany entered the war that was to become the First World War in 1914 on the 9th of Av (1 August according to the Gregorian calendar).

Also well-known is the designation of 9. 11. (November) according to the Gregorian/Julian calendar as the "Day of Fate" ("Schicksalstag der Deutschen"). Significant events that fall on 9/11 are:

1. 1918 November Revolution and proclamation of the Republic,
2. 1923 Beer Hall Putsch ("Hitler-Ludendorff Putsch"),
3. 1938 November pogroms ("Reichskristallnacht"),
4. 1989 Fall of the Berlin Wall, which was followed by the reunification of Germany.

From 1994 to 2019, four books about the German 9 November have been published. During this time, an interesting development took place about the meaning of 9/11. In 1994, Fritz Stern still said:

"The fact that four times in this century serious events in German history fell on the same day - 9 November - is a coincidence." [Stern 1994]

By 2019, the insight into the interconnections has deepened significantly. As Wolfgang Brenner notes:

"There is also an objective connection between the events of the Ninth of November. They all obey a historical logic. This logic is quite simple, namely causal. The ninth of November reacts to the ninth of November. There is an underlying connection between all these dates."[Brenner 2019]

Wherein this "objective connection" as well as the "underlying connection" consists and to what the 9/11 events refer to is explained in this book.

The results of the author's research:

The year 911 is also part of 9/11. In 911, Conrad I becomes king, on 9/11 (9 November). Conrad I is regarded as the first German king. With him the constructed name system of 31 kings begins, with 13 names in 403 years (31 x 13) until 1313 (see Hack #1).

King Louis, who died in 911, came from Upper Bavaria, as well as Louis, who was appointed king in 1314 (i.e. exactly in the year after the 403-year construction). Both are listed in official history as Louis IV.

On 9 November 1313, the Wittelsbach king Louis of Bavaria (Roman-German king from 1314) defeated the Habsburg Frederick the Fair (later the opposing king) in the Battle of Gammelsdorf. This victory established Louis' later supremacy in the empire. Wittelsbachers were kings in the empire in the 14th/15th and 18th centuries.

This provides the "objective connection" to the Ninth of November events of the 20th century, which otherwise stand completely unconnected. It begins on 9/ 11/ 911 with the first German King Conrad I.

The " underlying connection " is the reference to the 9th of Av (9/11) of the Jewish calendar, which is mentioned as an important date in the Torah. The setting of this day was done by God during the Exodus from Egypt on the 9th of Av (9/11) 1313 BC.

Furthermore, 9/11 (9 September, 9/11 read from the right) is the first day of the Coptic calendar (= new beginning), which goes back to the ancient Egyptian calendar. 9/11 (11/9 read from the right) is the 313rd day (read from the left and from the right) in the Gregorian calendar.

Pope Sylvester I (the one with the Donation of Constantine) became pope on 31/1/ 313, with a year beginning on 1/3 (1 March). He consecrated the Lateran Church (the highest-ranking papal basilica since then) on a 9/11 (324).

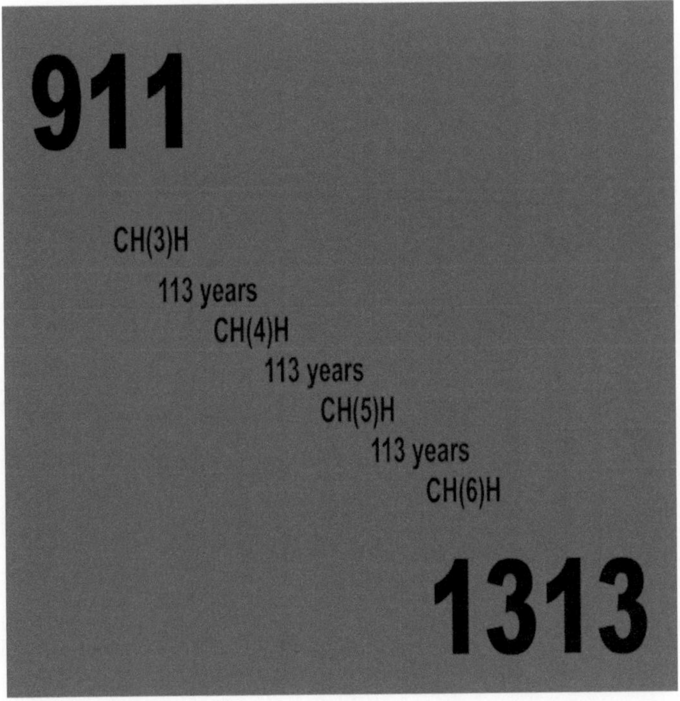

From Julius Caesar to Charles V

A series of important events in official history is arranged in 800-year intervals. Obviously, a basic framework of today's officially recognised chronology has thus been created at 800-year intervals.

In the year 800, exactly 800 years after the "Incarnation of the Lord" on 25 December, the Roman Empire emerges anew in the West with the coronation of Charlemagne as Emperor.

The biographical data of the two most important Roman rulers of antiquity, Julius Caesar and Augustus, are closely linked to those of the two most important Roman emperors of the Middle Ages and early modern times, Charles I, also known as the Great, and Charles V, "in whose empire the sun never set", and during whose reign Western Christianity in its present form came into being through the Reformation and Counter-Reformation.

Fig. 61-64: Julius Caesar, Augustus, Charlemagne und Charles V

Charles V was born 2 x 800 years after Julius Caesar, in 1500 AD, and ended his reign 2 x 800 years after him, in 1556 AD.

Charlemagne refers to Augustus, as he dies exactly 800 years after Augustus' death, in 814, and further biographical details are very similar after exactly 800 years.

E.G.: In 32 BC, Octavian had himself proclaimed "leader of Italy" and thus of the entire West. Charlemagne became king of the Frankish Empire exactly 800 years later, in 768.

In 27 BC, the civil war in Rome ended officially. The Roman Senate granted Octavian the title "Augustus".

Exactly 800 years later, in 773, Charlemagne is called to Italy by the Roman Pope, because of the Lombards once again. A year later, the Lombards were defeated, peace was restored and Charlemagne was crowned King of the Lombards in Italy.

According to another historical source, Charlemagne was born in 737, exactly 800 years after the birth of Emperor Augustus.

Official history says that Charlemagne's biographer Einhard was inspired by Suetonius, the ancient biographer of emperors, who also wrote about

Augustus. But when the dates follow such a clearly recognisable pattern as they do here, the boundary between historiography and pure fiction is crossed.

Charles V also clearly refers to Charlemagne (I). Both Charlemagne and Charles V were born in the year 1500. One was born ab 1500 urbe condita (= 747 AD), the other one 1500 Anno Domini. Thus their biographical dates are also linked via the era from the founding of the city of Rome - very appropriate for a Roman emperor.

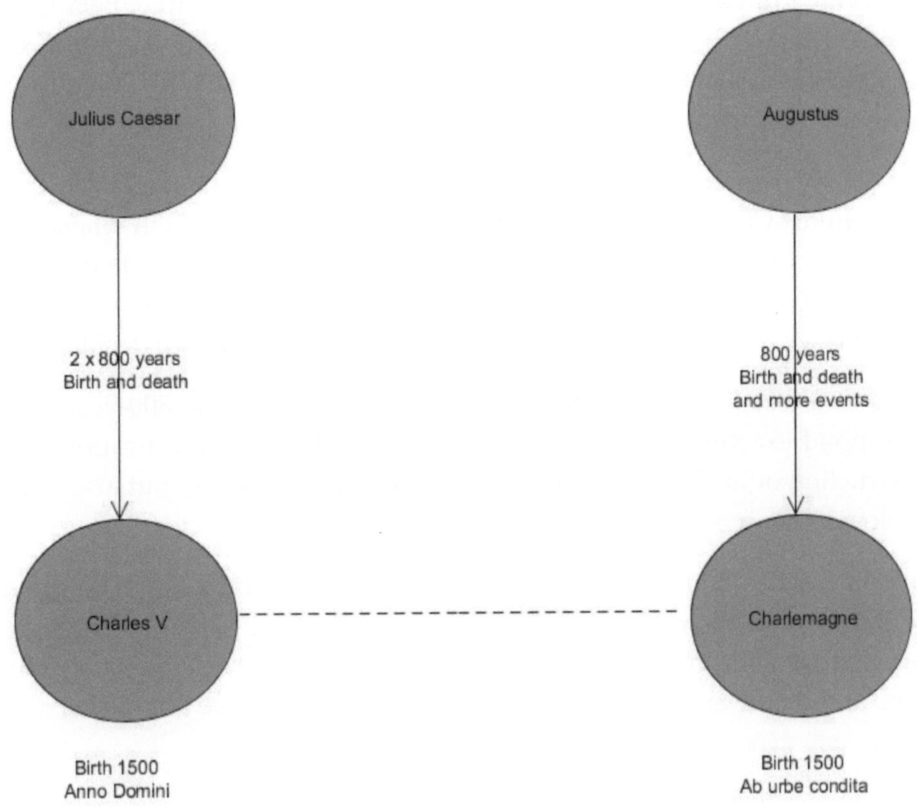

Fig. 65: The connection between the life dates of Julius Caesar, Augustus, Charlemagne and Charles V

The contradictory dates of Charlemagne's birth appearing in the written sources - either 737 or the most frequently mentioned year 747 (the year 742, which lies exactly in the middle, is also mentioned) - are either related to a construction with Emperor Augustus (737) or with Emperor Charles V (747). Either it fits with Augustus - exactly 800 years difference - or with Charles V - 1500 years since the foundation of the city of Rome (ab urbe condita).

Forging the biographical data of rulers, even by the rulers themselves, is still nothing unusual today. Only recently, in 2010, for example, Belarusian President Lukashenko changed his own date of birth in order to have the same birthday as his son. It would be a huge surprise if rulers of the distant past with incomparably greater powers had not done the same.

This 800-year interval concerns the most important Roman rulers in their epoch: Julius Caesar, Augustus, Charlemagne and Charles V, "in whose empire the sun never set". He was the last emperor to be re-crowned by the Roman Pope. This corresponds to Julius Caesar, who was the last ancient Roman ruler where Rome (the Senate) really had something to decide.

It has thus been proven that the biographical dates in the 800-year cycle correspond exactly. These are not merely parallelisms, but indications of a construction of history not only in the epistemological sense, but also in the ontological sense - a forgery.

This 800-year shift also affects the wars that were by far the most important for Germany in their epoch: the wars around the year of the beginning of the calendar with the Battle of the Teutoburg Forest, Charlemagne's Saxon Wars, and the devastating Eighty + Thirty Years War - more on this later.

From Troy via Rome to Constantinople

Furthermore, the main conquests of Rome (including Proto-Rome Troy and Nova Roma = Constantinople) that shape history occur at 800-year intervals.

Rome in Italy was conquered and sacked for the first time in 390 (other sources 387) BC, by the Celts (who are said by the authors not to have been separated from the Germanic tribes at that time).

After that there was the next conquest of Rome exactly 800 years later, in 410 by the Visigoths.

The first conquest of New Rome (the Greek Constantinople) took place in 1204, exactly 796 years later, by the Franks or Latins from Western Europe.

And since the Romans derive their origin from Troy, we can include Troy as the proto-Rome, so to speak. According to Eratosthenes' data, Troy was conquered by the Greeks in 1184 BC, exactly 794 years before Rome was taken by the Celts.

So we have four conquests of Rome that change further history, each 800 years apart (deviation < 1%). The first begins with a victory of the Greeks and a defeat of the Trojans (from whom Rome is said to have been founded in Italy and the Franks are said to be descended). The last one ends with a victory of the Franks and Latins (with the Roman Pope) over the Greeks. And so the circle closes.

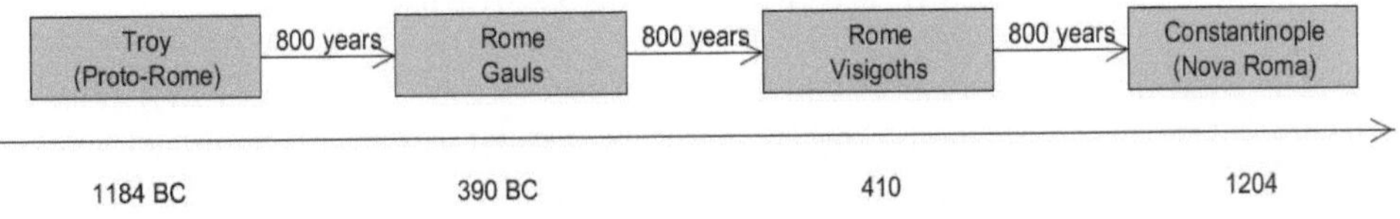

Fig. 66: Conquests of Rome that shape history, 800 years apart

Fig. 67 (left): Troy being conquered by the Greeks, 1184 BC
Fig. 68 (right): The sack of Rome by Brennus and the Celts in 390 BC

Fig. 69 (left): The conquest of Rome by Alaric and the Visigoths in 410 AD
Fig. 70 (right): The conquest of Constantinople by the Crusaders in 1204

Three wars in and around the Teutoburg Forest

There is also a war every 800 years with reference to the Teutoburg Forest. In the year 9, in written sources, the so-called Battle of the Teutoburg Forest takes place, as part of the wars between Romans and Germanic tribes at the beginning of our era.

800 years later, the Saxon Wars of Charlemagne (772-804) take place, beginning in the Teutoburg Forest.

And 800 years after that, there is the Eighty Years' War+Thirty Years' War (1568-1648), which is brought to an end by the Peace of Westphalia in Osnabrück (Teutoburg Forest).

Fig. 71: Three wars in and around the Teutoburg Forest 800 years apart

But there are other significant events that are pretty much 800 years apart.

On the Iberian Peninsula

The Iberian peninsula also knows the 800-year cycle: if you look at the history of the peninsula from 1500, 700 and 100 BC, you can see:

1500: The Reconquista was completed eight years ago, in 1492. In the same year, the Jews were expelled by the Alhambra Edict, unless they allowed themselves to be compulsorily baptised.

700: For some decades now, the Eastern Romans have been expelled from the peninsula - by the Visigoths. For a long time, the Eastern Romans still occupied almost the same territory (Granada) that had remained to the Muslims even before the later final victory of the Spaniards. And almost exactly 800 years before the Alhambra edict, the Council of Toledo took place in 694, at which the Visigothic king demanded the extermination of Judaism with expulsion and enslavement.

Another 800 years back, in 100 BC, the Romans had just conquered most of the Iberian Peninsula. Only a small part of the north of the peninsula is not yet occupied. Curiously, this is precisely the part of the peninsula that was later never occupied by the Muslims, and would become the starting point of the Reconquista.

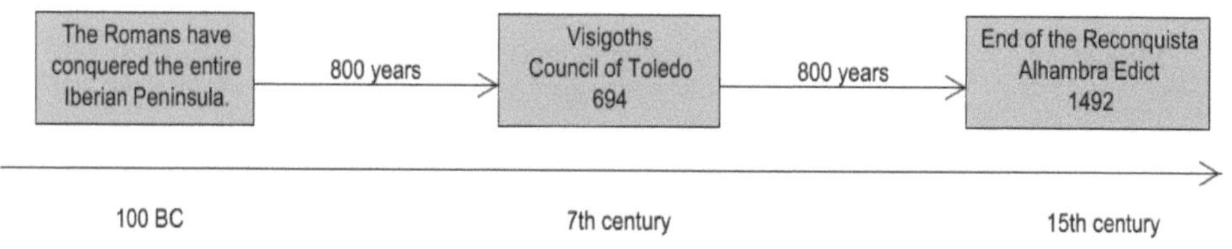

Fig. 72: Three events, each 800 years apart, on the Iberian Peninsula

Of Russians, Swedes and Goths

The following three events are also about 800 years apart:

1)
Between 1655-1661, the Second Northern War took place, mainly on the territory of Poland-Lithuania. At that time, this also included Belarus and western Ukraine. The Polish king (great-grandson of the Swedish King Gustav I) claimed the Swedish throne for a time; between 1592-1599 there was actually a Swedish king on the Polish throne. This war is also called the "Swedish Flood" in Poland.

2)
In the "Nestor's chronicle" (also called "Tale of Bygone Years" or "Primary Chronicle") about the events exactly 800 years earlier we read the following:

Scandinavian settlements on the territory of present-day Russia and Ukraine since about 750.

854: Prince Rurik from Sweden arrives in Kiev.

862: Locals and Varangians fight with each other. The Varangians are expelled. However, there is no peace. Afterwards, a delegation of Slavs travels to Sweden and invites the Varangians to rule over the quarrelling tribes.

In 882, Kievan Rus is founded by Helgi (Oleg). Thereafter, there is further fighting until the first half of the 10th century.

Even after the Second Northern War, 800 years later, the fighting does not stop. The Great Northern War follows between 1700 and 1722. The Swedes occupied parts of the Ukraine and Russia. In 1709, there were widespread uprisings against the Swedish occupation.

3)
If we go back 800 years again from the beginning of the 10th century, i.e. to the beginning of the second century, we see Goths entering Ukraine from Poland during that time. Originally, the Goths are said to have come from Sweden. The Swedish king also officially called himself "King of the Swedes, Goths and Vandals" until 1973.

Fig. 73: Three events, each 800 years apart, in Eastern Europe (Russia/Ukraine/Poland)

Of plagues, Huns and Mongols

The greatest plague of antiquity, the Justinian Plague, began in Constantinople in 542. After that, there were repeated outbreaks of the plague in the following 150 years.

The greatest plague of the Middle Ages, the Black Death, broke out exactly 805 years later, in 1347, in Constantinople, and then spread across almost all of Europe. More outbreaks follow in the next 150 years.

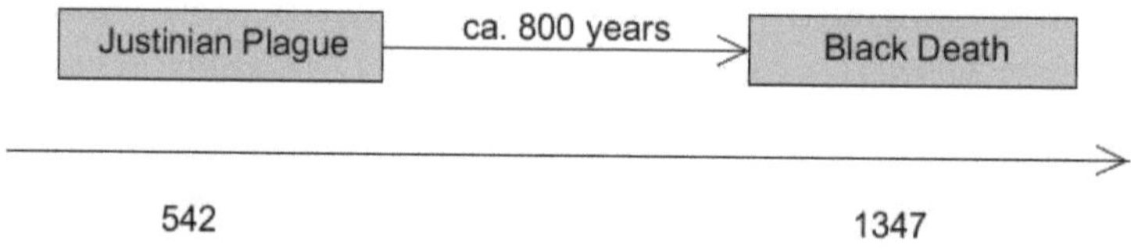

Fig. 74: The largest plagues at intervals of approx. 800 years

The Huns were defeated in the battle of the Catalaunian Plains in 451. The Mongols allegedly did not get quite as far 790 years later - it is said to have ended after just one year on the Adriatic.

The conquests of the Huns and Mongols, 800 years apart, also match up well geographically. They invaded not only China and Europe, but also India and Persia. Older historians still referred to the Huns of antiquity as Mongols.

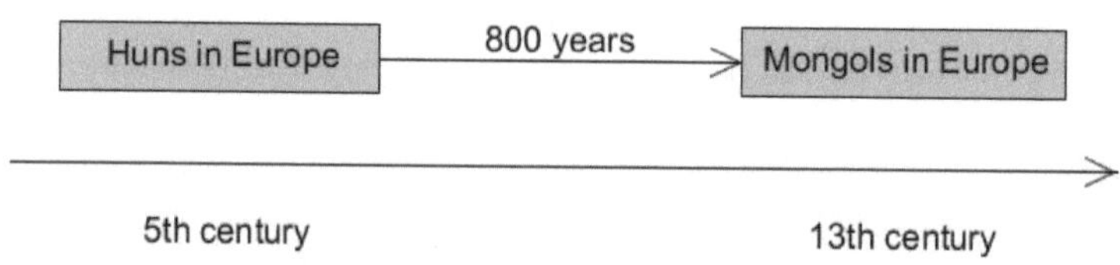

Fig. 75: The cavalry armies of the Huns and Mongols at an interval of approx. 800 years

Charles' absence in the High Middle Ages

The first Carolingian is considered to be Charles Martel (c. 688 - 741), who from 715 was the mayor of the palace (head of the administration) of the sub-kingdom of Austrasia and from 718 the mayor of the palace of the entire kingdom and thus the de facto ruler of the Frankish kingdom. Charles Martel is the first ruler with the name Charles that is documented in written sources.

Charlemagne was then the second ruler and first king of the Carolingians from 768. In 800 he was crowned emperor by the Pope in Rome. He was followed by other Kings of the Carolingian dynasty named Charles.

Emperor Charles III (876-887), the Fat, was the last Carolingian king named Charles in the East Frankish Empire. The last Carolingian king ever named

Charles was Charles III (898-923), the Simple, king of the West Frankish Empire. At the beginning of the 11th century, the dynasty of the Carolingians ended in male legitimate line.

The next French-born king with the name Charles was Charles I of Anjou (1226-1285), King of Sicily from the Capetian dynasty, more than 300 years later. He is considered to be the last-born son of the French King Louis VIII (1187-1226), although the exact circumstances of his birth are disputed.

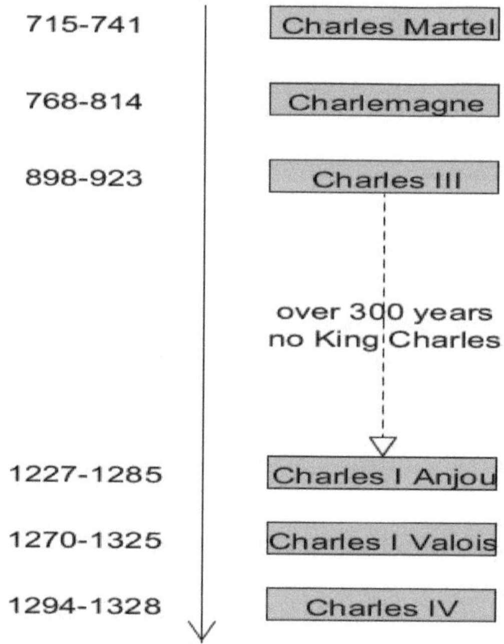

Fig. 76: From Charles Martel to Charles IV with over 300 years without a Charles

In the East Franconian and Roman-German noble houses, not only was there not a single king named Charles during the High Middle Ages, no, not a single member of a ruling dynasty has the name Charles. Not a single Conradine, Ottone, Salian, Guelph, Nassau, Wittelsbach, Habsburg, Luxembourg or Hohenstaufen, etc., has the name Charles until the Roman-German King Charles IV (born 1316).

The name Charles is missing after the Carolingian kings in the 10th century, which is inexplicable for official history. And this even with a popular, Germanic name, which Charles is supposed to be according to official history!

Prior to the author, only A. Bach noticed the strange absence of the name Charles (Karl) after the early Middle Ages. Among the 1000 students of the University of Cologne in the 14th and 15th centuries, for example, he does not find a single Charles (Karl) [Bach 1943, p. 351].

Until the beginning of the 17th century, the name Charles seems to have been given only sporadically. Bach can only detect a growing popularity of the name Charles after 1610, following the canonisation of another Charles, the Cardinal of Milan Charles Borromeo.

Charlemagne was both king and emperor as well as a saint (canonised by the Catholic Church). So why is his name found so late after the end of the Carolingians?

The doubled Charles as an error of chronology

1.) King Charles I of the Franks, also called "the Great", dies in 814, and King Charles I of Anjou, also called "the Great", also regent of France, dies in 1285 (distance 471 years).

2.) King Charles I of the Franks, also called "the Great", is crowned by the Pope in Rome at Christmas 800, and King Charles I of Anjou, also called "the Great", also Regent of France, is crowned by the Pope in Rome at (orthodox) Christmas 1266 (466 years apart).

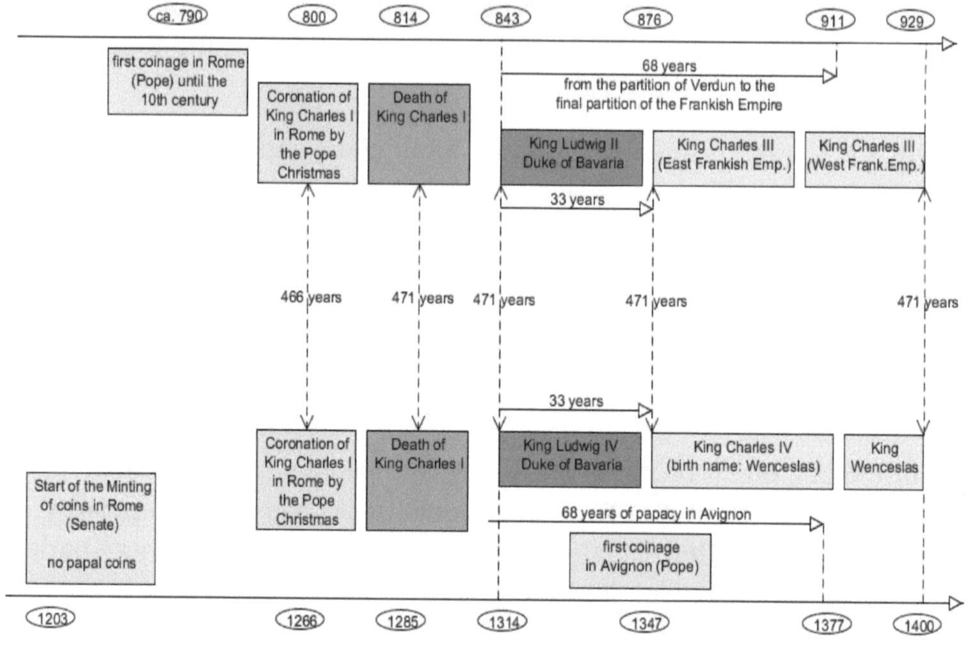

Fig. 77: The parallels at 466/471 year intervals in the 8th-10th and 13th-14th centuries. Above Rome/Italy and Frankish Empire, below Rome/Italy and Holy Roman Empire

After the division of the Frankish Empire in 843, Louis from Bavaria reigned as East Frankish king for 33 years (called Louis II, the German), with a successor named Charles. And from 1314, Louis from Bavaria reigns as Roman-German king for 33 years, with a successor named Charles. There are also 471 years between 843 and 1314.

This leads to the suspicion that the two Kings Charles and the two Kings Louis of Bavaria could be the same person. Other parallels are also important - see Fig. 77.

These parallels end in the Frankish Empire in 929, when the West Frankish king Charles III dies. This is also exactly when the French system of royal names begins with the 3 x 131 years (see Hack #1).

Exactly 471 years later, in 1400, the Roman-German king Wenceslas was deposed. This is a namesake of his predecessor Charles IV, whose birth name was also Wenceslas. Interestingly, King Charles III, who lived 471 years earlier, was also deposed, six years before his death.

One year before Ludwig IV became king, in 1313, the Roman-German system of kings' names, which began in 911, came to an end (see Hack #1). The king who reigned before that was also a Louis from Bavaria, also numbered IV.

Furthermore, there are other striking parallels in a similar time interval [Arndt 2020/1], also in Ethiopian history. For the Ethiopian history, O. Neugebauer had already proven an error in the chronology. In Ethiopian history, dates of identical rulers are repeated at intervals of 456 years.

"Of central importance is the fact that for many Ethiopian dates of rulers there are two very different dates, always 456 years apart." [Neugebauer, S. 55]

If we consider a different year for the creation of the world than assumed in the previous calculations, the Ethiopian error of chronology also results in a difference of 471 years.

In Hack #2 it was shown that the most important calendar eras of antiquity are coordinated according to a clear plan. The number 529 plays a decisive role in this.

The dating of the years of death of Charlemagne (814) and Charles I of Anjou (1285), which differ by 471 years, as well as the beginning of the reign of King Louis II (843) and King Louis IV (1314), results from the numbers 529 and 1000 as follows:

814 + 1000 – 529 = 1285 resp. 1285 – 1000 + 529 = 814, und
843 + 1000 – 529 = 1314 resp. 1314 – 1000 + 529 = 843.

All these doublings at intervals of 456-476 years obviously have their cause in the construction of calendar eras and thus chronology - Hack #2.

In some countries, these duplicates were then given written sources so that they now appear as two different persons/events in the history books of official history, such as Charlemagne and Charles I of Anjou. This did not happen in Ethiopia, for example, so that today no one doubts that they are one and the same person and the duplication is only a chronological error.

Charles I of Valois

Charles I of Valois (1270-1325) is the progenitor of the House of Valois, and thus of all the kings of France from 1328 (Philip VI) to 1589. According to official history, he was (titular) Emperor of Constantinople, (titular) King of Aragon, temporary Regent of France, as well as Governor in Italy, etc. He gladly and often waged war in all the territories mentioned. This is a common characteristic of him and Charlemagne as well as Charles I of Anjou.

The great-grandmother of Charles I of Valois was called Blanche and came from Spain (both grandfather and great-grandfather are called Louis). According to the legend of "Flor and Blancheflor", Blancheflor was the grandmother of Charlemagne and came from Spain.

Blanche of Castile was the wife of King Louis the Lion (1187-1226), with whom, according to official history, the Carolingian revival began - and he became the father of the first Charles. Blanche is the mother of Charles I of Anjou, the first Charles after the Carolingians, who is thus great uncle of Charles I of Valois. Charles Martell, the first Carolingian, was the grandfather of Charlemagne.

This statue of Charles I of Valois (1270-1325) is an excellent match for the Carolus coins:

Fig.. 78: Head of the statue of Charles I of Valois (tomb) in St Denis

Fig. 79: Silver denier, Image of KAROLUS IMP AVG (attributed to Charlemagne)

Fig. 80: Charlemagne by Albrecht Dürer (1510). This image differs from later fantasy and ideal images, but corresponds perfectly to the portraits on the coins attributed to Charlemagne and the statue of Charles of Valois

Charles I of Anjou

Charles I of Anjou (1227-1285), on the other hand, looks deceptively like Charles Martel. He has an edgy face in contrast to the round face of Charles I of Valois and Charles I the Great (Charlemagne). Even the nose and chin are practically the same shape, if you think away the beard. Interestingly, even the haircut is identical.

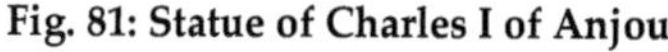

Fig. 81: Statue of Charles I of Anjou

Fig. 82: Head of the statue of CharlesMartell in St Denis (tomb)

There was also another Charles of Anjou in the 13th century, with the name Charles Martel (1271-1295), according to official history grandson of Charles I (perhaps identical with him?). He was also king of Sicily and crowned king of Hungary, but could not establish himself there, so that today he is only considered a Hungarian titular king.

In Hungarian written sources, Charles I of Anjou, the grandfather of Charlemagne, is called "Carolus Magnus", i.e. "Charlemagne" [Archiv 1900, p. 437]. In the 9th century, Charles Martel is the grandfather of Charlemagne, i.e. the other way round.

Charles I of Anjou was the most powerful ruler in Europe of his time and is sometimes referred to by historians as the "uncrowned emperor of the Occident".

The phantom reflections

The king (REX) and emperor (IMP AVG) Charles I of Valois (1270-1325), the progenitor of all French kings after him until 1589, and his great-uncle Charles I of Anjou (REX, the first French-born king named Charles) are thus the models for Charlemagne and Charles Martel, the first Charles ever and grandfather of Charlemagne.

These are phantom reflections in the sense of the history analyst A. Fomenko [Fomenko 2003]. The back projection of the dates of Charles I of Anjou and Charles I of Valois to Charles Martel and Charlemagne was not always done 1:1. As is well known, even in historiography, Charles Martel and Charlemagne are not always sharply separated. Charles Martel is also referred to as king (rex) in some written sources.

Two important dates in the life of Charles I of Anjou match the 466/471 year difference to Charlemagne, the coronation and the death. In physical appearance, however, he is extremely similar to Charles Martel, while at the same time Charles I of Valois looks strikingly similar to Charlemagne on the coins and the Dürer painting of 1510, and was also (titular) emperor (IMP AVG).

The father of (titular) Emperor Charles I of Valois was called Philip, and so was his eldest son. The father of Charlemagne was called Pippin (Pepin), and so was his eldest son.

According to the author, Pippin (Pepin) is simply an Old French short form of Philip (similar to the Italian short form Pippo).

Charlemagne I of Valois also had a mother named Elizabeth (Isabella), which is quite similar to "Bertha", Charlemagne's mother (modern Slavic short forms of Elizabeth e.g. "Beta"). The (great) grandmother Blanche(flor) from Spain of both has already been mentioned. In the case of the not quite identical names, it should be noted that the spelling of names was not standardised in these times.

Military campaigns in France, Italy and Spain have been documented for Charles I of Anjou and Charles I of Valois as well as for Charlemagne, so that the phantom reflections match here.

Charles I of Anjou made several crusades to the Holy Land. Interestingly, however, there are also several written sources in which it is reported that Charlemagne had made one or two crusades to the Holy Land.

However, these written sources for Charlemagne are not recognised by official history today and the historian J. Fried speaks of an "implanted memory". The phantom reflection of Charles I of Anjou on Charlemagne does not suit official history here.

	Charlemagne	Charles I of Valois	Charles I of Anjou
Father	Pippin	Philip (for short Pippin)	
Mother	Bertha	Elisabeth (for short Beta)	
Eldest son	Pippin	Philipp (for short Pippin)	
(Great-)Grandmother	Blancheflor from Spain	Blanche from Spain	
Image	Identical	Identical	
Kriegsherr und Titelsammler	Identical	Identical	Identical
First King Charles	First King Charles		First King Charles (after the Carolingians)
called "the Great"	"the Great"		"the Great"
Coronation in Rome by the Pope at Christmas	800		(orthodox) 1266 (466 years later)
Death	814		1285 (471 years later)

Table 11: The make up of Charlemagne's biographical data

The Carolingians and Biblical Israel

The stories about Charlemagne and his predecessors and successors have obviously been constructed with reference to biblical Israel. The period of the first three Carolingian kings Pippin, Charles and Louis has been inspired by the Old Testament books of Samuel and 1 Kings, and thus the first three kings of Israel before the partition: Saul, David and Solomon.

A. Fomenko [Fomenko 2003] had already compared the kings of the kingdoms of Israel and Judah after the partition of Israel around 931 BC and the kings of the Holy Roman Empire from the 10th - 13th centuries. However, he did not cover the Carolingian period before that or only saw it in connection with the ancient Roman period [Fomenko 2003, p. 280 ff].

It is not new that Charlemagne compared the Franks to the ancient Israelites and saw himself as the new David. He even had himself addressed as "new David" at court. But the actual parallels go beyond that, and look more like a historical construction.

As the first ruler of Israel, Saul is anointed by the highest priest. The first three kings of Israel were Saul, David and Solomon (= the peaceful one). This was followed by the division of the kingdom.

As the first ruler of the Carolingians, Pippin is anointed by the highest priest (Pope). Among the Carolingians, the first three kings were Pippin, Charles and Louis the Pious. After that, the division of the empire followed.

So we have here an identical structuring of the history of Israel from King Saul via King David and Solomon to the division of the empire after Solomon's death and of the Carolingian empire from Pippin via Charles and Louis to the division of the empire after Louis' death.

In addition, there are other parallels, which are covered in more detail in Table 12.

Table 12: Comparison of Israel and the Carolingian Empire/Holy Roman Empire

Israel	Carolingian dynasty and Holy Roman Empire	Comments
1. King Saul	1. King Pippin	Ritually anointed as the first king of Israel / of the Carolingian dynasty in the Frankish Empire
Esbaal is king in the north for a short time	Carloman is king in the south for a short time	"Minor division" of the kingdom, which is only short-term and of no significance, after the death of the first king
2. King David (= Darling)	2. King Charlemagne (Carolus = Darling = David); he compared himself with David, but also to Josiah = Charles I of Anjou according to Fomenko	Great Warriors; Expansion of the empire and peak of power; Role models for later kings
3. King Solomon (= the Peaceful)	3. King Louis the Pious	Consolidation and legislation
Building of the Temple in Jerusalem	Building of the Palatine Chapel in Aachen	Construction of a symbolically important sacred building within approx. 7 years
Saul => Solomon: 1079 - 931 BC	Pippin => Louis: 751 - 840 (911) AD (Louis IV 900-911)	Pagan elements are still present; relapse into old customs; apostasy from the correct faith
Approx. 931 BC Division of the Empire Israel and Judah	843 AD Division of the Empire (911 AD final division) West and East Frankish Empire	After the death of the 3rd king, division of the Empire
931 BC – 597 BC	843 / 911 AD – 1309 AD	Period from the division of the Empire to the Babylonian Captivity; 3 x 113 years in the Holy Roman Empire as well as 3 x 131 years in France; in 403 years 31 kings with 13 names: 31 x 13 = 403
597 – 539 BC Babylonian Exile, also called Babylonian Captivity	1309 – 1377 AD Papal See in Avignon, also called Babylonian Captivity	Babylonian Captivity

Emperor Augustus and Charlemagne

The striking features of the structuring of the biographical data of Emperor Augustus and Charlemagne at 800-year intervals have already been discussed in Hack #4.

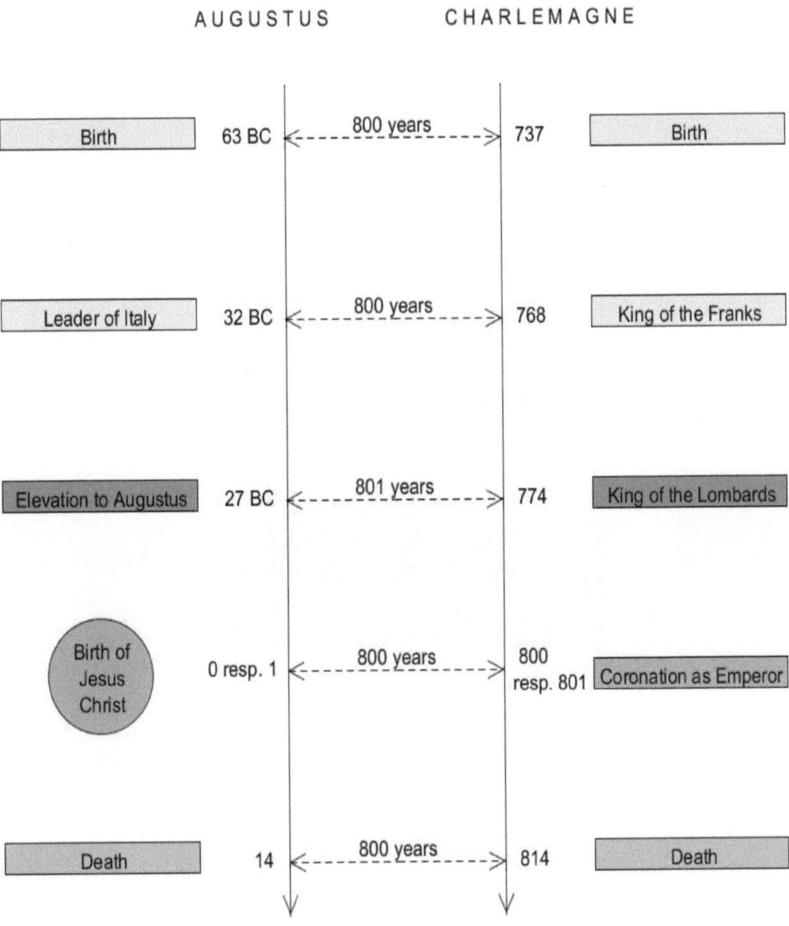

Fig. 83: The lives of Emperor Augustus and Charlemagne with important events 800 years apart. And in addition, the birth of Jesus Christ.

Sources for the fictional character of history "Charlemagne"

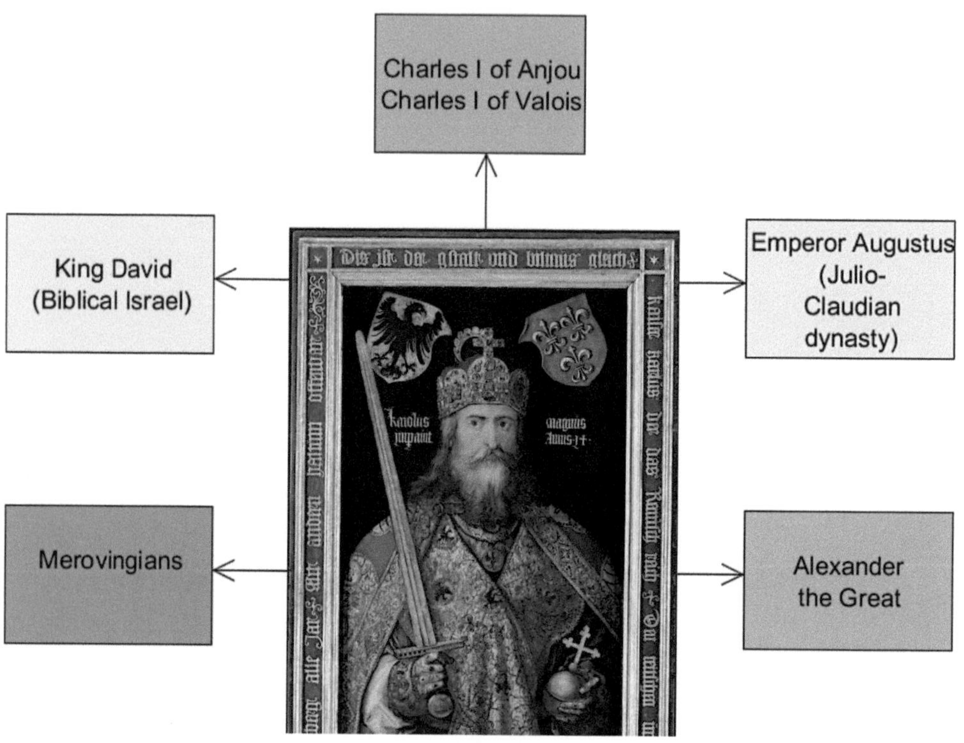

The constructed Dates of the Julian-Claudian Dynasty

It is now over 2000 years since one of the most popular figures in official history died: "Emperor Augustus".

But what is the myth of "Emperor Augustus" all about?

Fig. 85: Emperor Augustus (63 BC - 14 AD), the first emperor of the Roman Empire. His most important biographical data are arranged in the official history exactly 800 years before Charlemagne (see also Hack #4 and Hack #5).

Fig. 86: Emperor Augustus in Las Vegas. He is said to have written an autobiography. However, this has been "lost". Instead, we have the *"The Deeds of the Divine Augustus"* (*Res gestae divi Augusti*), an obnoxious work of propaganda. This "report of deeds" is said to have been a funerary inscription, which is claimed to have been written by Emperor Augustus himself. However, this epitaph has not survived. Only three copies of it have survived. The first was "discovered" in Turkey in the middle of the 16th century by order of the Roman-German Emperor Charles V, two others in the 19th century, also in Turkey.

In Roman history there are two assassinations of a ruler named Gaius Julius Caesar (both times with many daggers), both organised by a certain Cassius, which were followed by the attempt to renew the Republic by the Roman Senate.

One is the dictator known as "Caesar" (100 - 44 BC). The other one is the emperor known today as "Caligula" from 37 - 41 A.D. This seems to be a duplication of only one event. Yes, even the entire 84/85 years from 44 BC - 41 AD are obviously a doubling - an entire Roman Easter cycle.

The conspicuities in the biographical data of the rulers of this period are too great to be coincidental. The biographical data look rather fabricated.

This concerns on the one hand the Julians (all named Gaius Julius Caesar) and on the other hand the Claudians (all named Tiberius Claudius Nero), who together with the emperor known as "Nero" form the Julian-Claudian dynasty.

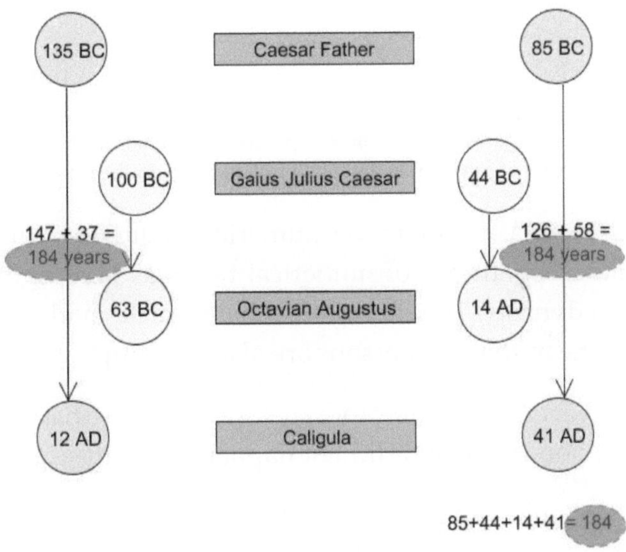

Fig. 87: The quite obviously constructed biographical data of the Julians - years of birth on the left and years of death on the right

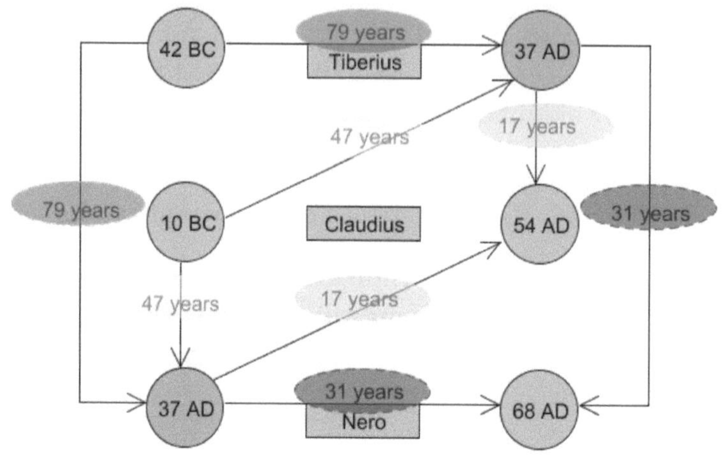

79 + 31 = 110 = 42 + 68

Fig. 88: The even more obviously made-up biographical data of the Claudians - years of birth on the left and years of death on the right

In the case of "naturally" occurring numerical sequences, there cannot be such conspicuous repetitions of numerical ratios as here in the case of the Julian-Claudian dynasty. The dates must therefore be made up, which does not necessarily mean that the persons are also made up.

In addition, however, there are other historical events that were obviously created at the scribe's desk and did not happen in reality, e.g.:

Tiberius and Caligula reign successively for a total of 27 years (14 - 41). Then Caligula is murdered, with daggers.

Afterwards, Claudius and Nero reign successively for a total of 27 years (41 - 68). Then Nero kills himself with a dagger with the help of his servant, as he would otherwise have been murdered - thus quasi forced suicide.

After the four-emperor year 68, Vespasian, Titus (according to [Pfister 2019] identical with Vespasian) and Domitian reign successively for a total of 27 years (69 - 96). Then Domitian is assassinated, with a dagger.

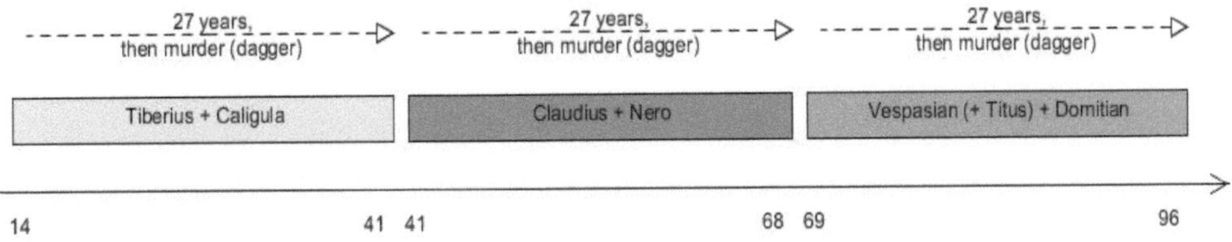

Fig. 89: The first century AD - Every 27 years there is an assassination of an emperor with daggers

This is primarily about events that are known from the work of the ancient historiographer Suetonius. In his biographies of the emperors ("De vita Caesarum"), Suetonius (51 - 96 AD) describes the twelve Roman rulers from Gaius Julius Caesar to Domitian, i.e. the period from 100 BC to 96 AD. These events quite obviously could not have taken place as they are written in the history books.

Further structuring of the history of the Roman Empire

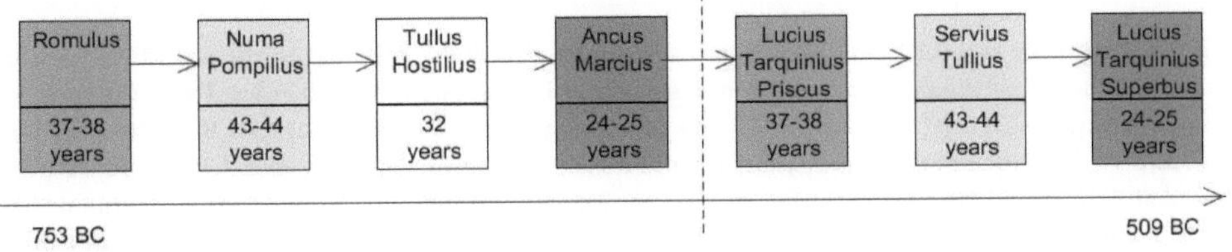

Fig. 90: The reigns of the Roman kings from 753 - 509 BC are regularly repeated.

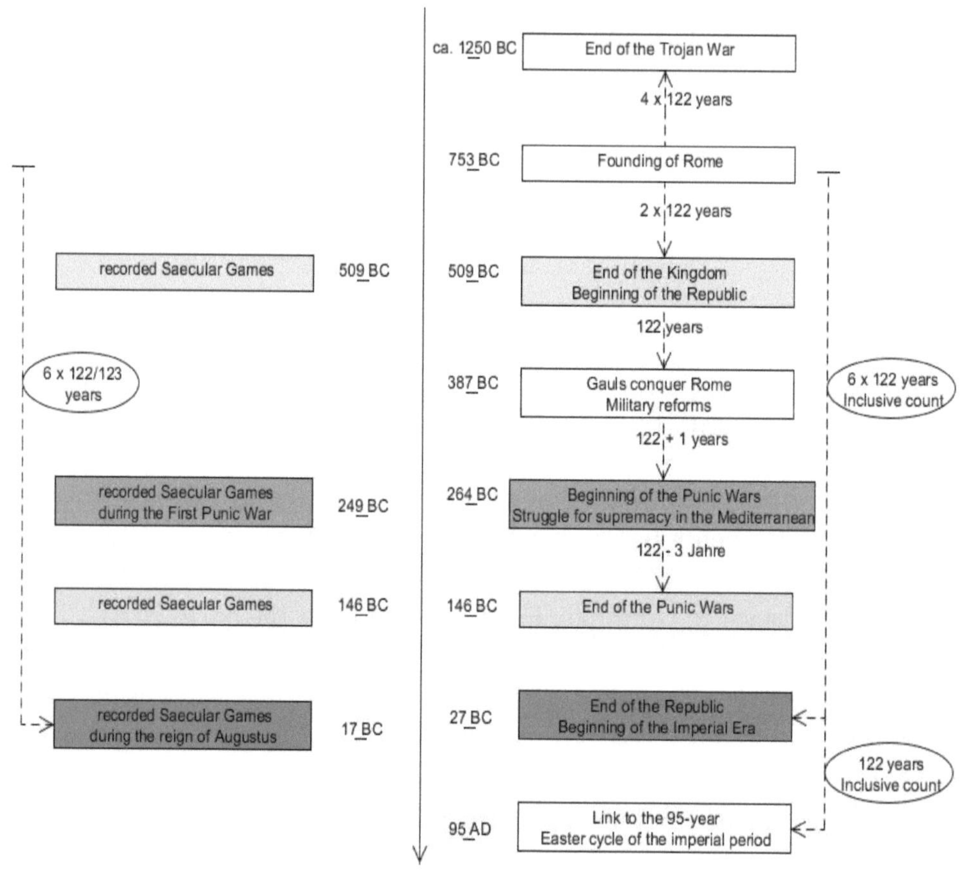

Fig. 91: In Roman antiquity, so-called Saecular Games were held, oriented to the founding year of Rome (753 BC). Traditionally, the length of a saeculum is assumed to be 110 years. Up to the time of Emperor Augustus, only four Saecular Games have been recorded, in the years 509 B.C., 249 B.C., 146 B.C. and 17 B.C. None of these four years fit into the 110-year grid - not even close! The author's proposed structuring of the Roman period in 122-year intervals (right) and the perfectly matching recorded Saecular Games up to Augustus. No other Saecular Games have been recorded up to Augustus. 122 years = 95 + 27 years. We will encounter these dates again in a moment.

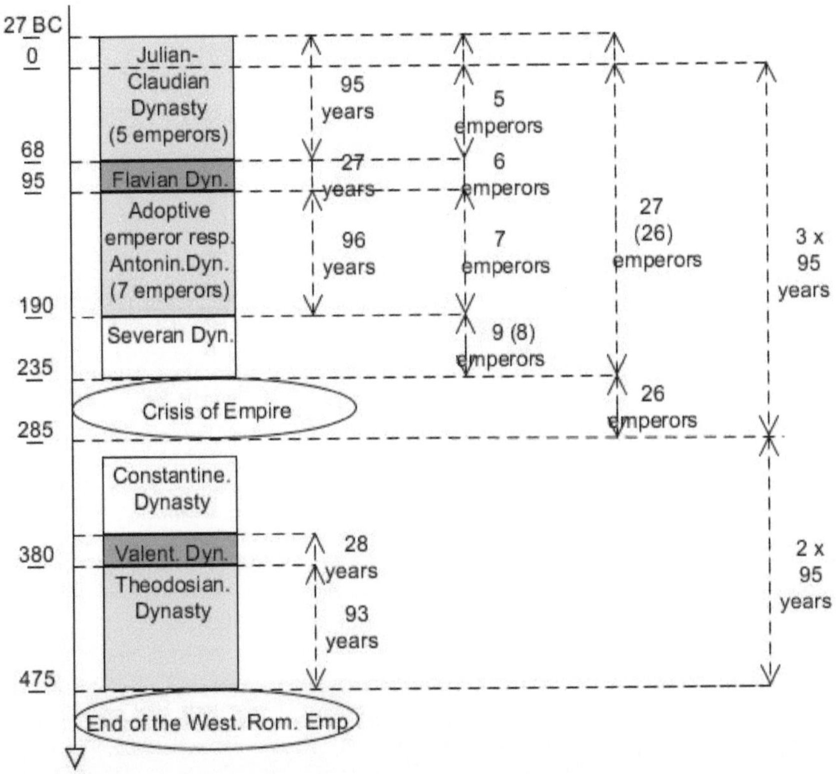

Fig. 92: The structuring of the Roman imperial period until the end of the Western Roman Empire. Included are the legitimate emperors and the co-emperors of equal rank. On the left of the timeline are the steps of 95 and two other important dates. The two emperor numbers in brackets are the ideal value, the numbers without brackets those according to official history.

Until the end of the Western Empire in 476, there were a total of seven imperial dynasties in the Roman Empire, as well as a lot of other emperors. In each of the years of the 95 year intervals (+/- 2), a new imperial dynasty came to power or an old one came to an end:

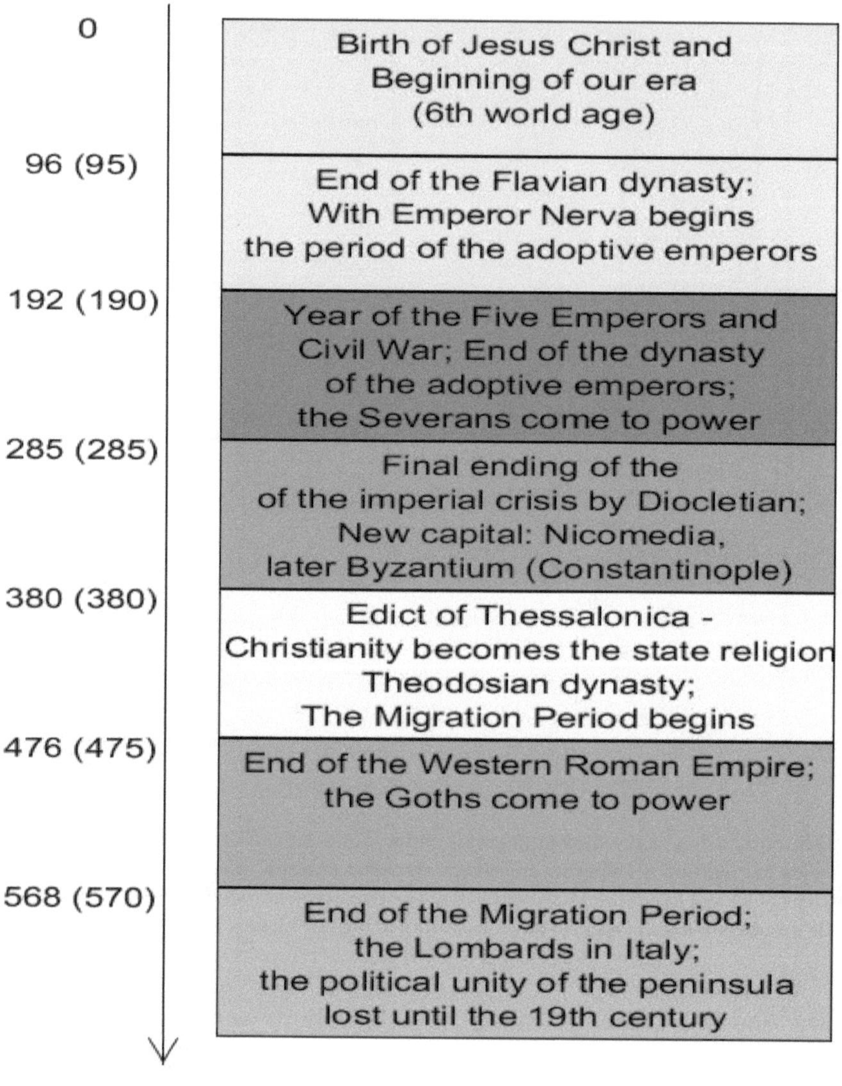

0	Birth of Jesus Christ and Beginning of our era (6th world age)
96 (95)	End of the Flavian dynasty; With Emperor Nerva begins the period of the adoptive emperors
192 (190)	Year of the Five Emperors and Civil War; End of the dynasty of the adoptive emperors; the Severans come to power
285 (285)	Final ending of the of the imperial crisis by Diocletian; New capital: Nicomedia, later Byzantium (Constantinople)
380 (380)	Edict of Thessalonica - Christianity becomes the state religion Theodosian dynasty; The Migration Period begins
476 (475)	End of the Western Roman Empire; the Goths come to power
568 (570)	End of the Migration Period; the Lombards in Italy; the political unity of the peninsula lost until the 19th century

Fig. 93: The structuring of the history of the Roman Empire into seven Easter cycles of 95 years each since the birth of Jesus Christ (in brackets the exact number of the 95 Easter cycles), which obviously was created at the scribe's desk.

Chronology and astronomy

The founder of scientific chronology, Joseph Justus Scaliger (1540-1609), already made use of astronomy and was in contact with astronomers who supported him in his calculations, including Johannes Kepler (1571-1630), the discoverer of the planetary laws. These calculations served to link astronomical events, primarily solar and lunar eclipses, with historical events and thus chronology. Astronomy was and is therefore an important field for the establishment of a valid, generally recognised chronology.

However, there was neither freedom of speech nor academic freedom at that time or before (according to official history, only with a few exceptions, which is also highly doubtful). It is therefore completely unclear whether the chronology established at that time, and still valid today, with Jesus Christ at the beginning of our era, has anything to do with reality, the actual past.

Fig. 94 (left): Johannes Kepler and Fig. 95 (right): Joseph Justus Scaliger - The Dream Team of Chronology

It could just as well have been decreed by the rulers of that time, e.g. in the sense of anchoring the Christian religion in history, with Jesus Christ in the middle of time, just as Jerusalem was in the middle of the world according to the beliefs of that time.

I quote H. Fuhrmann, the former president of the "Monumenta Germaniae Historica" (German Institute for the Study of the Middle Ages):

"But when a doctrine is decreed by holders of ruling power, then that can happen what we know from the closed society of the Middle Ages and the totalitarianism of modern times: the search for truth is directed. It is not the question of authenticity or inauthenticity that determines the truth and relevance of a writing, but its conformity to doctrine. In George Orwell's novel "1984", one of the only four ministries of the totalitarian state is the "Ministry of Truth", which watches over the corpus of knowledge and determines the truth."

[Fuhrmann 1988, Preface to MGH Tome 33.I.]

Since the establishment of the chronology used today took place with the help of astronomy, a criticism of chronology cannot lead to valid results without adequate consideration of the most important astronomical events here - solar and lunar eclipses.

This assignment of astronomical events, especially of solar and lunar eclipses, to the time axis, the chronology, found by Scaliger, results exclusively from the eclipse reports (considered genuine without proof), their chronological classification according to official history and their scientifically questionable interpretation.

This assignment may match for a part of the eclipse reports, but by no means for all of them, since besides the inaccuracy of the records, the share of subsequently added, back-calculated and literary eclipses in the written sources is unknown. The historian A. Demandt remarks on this:

"Of the 250 or so reports in ancient literature about solar and lunar eclipses, over 200 are inaccurate or false." [Demandt, S. 469]

The problem with the assignment of official history is that it only works if strong, arbitrary fluctuations of the Earth's rotation in the early Middle Ages and in antiquity are used in the calculations. These fluctuations in the Earth's rotation create deviations of Universal Time from Terrestrial Time, called Delta T, which affect the visibility of calculated eclipses. More on this later.

On the solar eclipse of 16 June 364, observed by Theon of Alexandria, the British astronomer F. Richard Stephenson (* 1941) writes:

"It is still the only solar eclipse for which careful measurements of time are available from ancient Europe " [Stephenson 1997, S. 365]

To be more precise than Stephenson: <u>Not a single</u> solar eclipse from ancient Europe has come down to us with measured time and further details, and can thus be verified to some extent, since the observation took place in Alexandria (Egypt), which, as we know, is not in Europe.

Example: Thucydides' three eclipses in the Peloponnesian War

The problem of assigning recorded eclipse reports to calculated eclipses will be illustrated in the following with an example (a very well-known one at that).

The Greek historian Thucydides mentioned three eclipses in his description of the first twenty years of the Peloponnesian War (431 - 404 BC) (quoted by [Gautschy, p. 5/6]).

These are two solar eclipses at intervals of 7 years and a lunar eclipse 11 years after the second solar eclipse. An exact date is not mentioned.

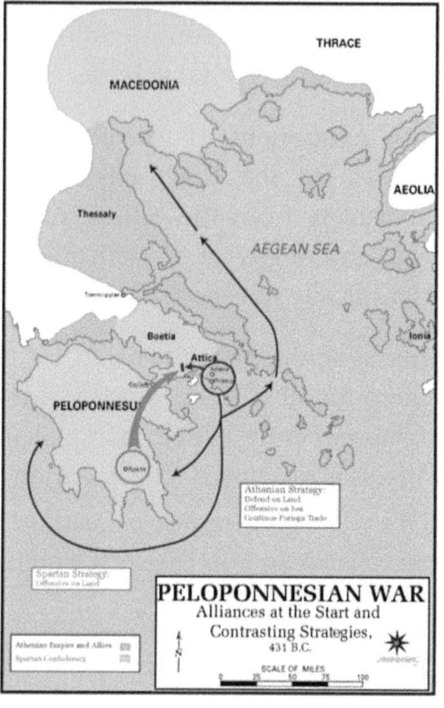

Fig. 96: The opponents of the Peloponnesian War: Athens and the Attic Sea League (orange) and Sparta with the Peloponnesian League (green). In the end, green won.

The first solar eclipse was observed after noon in the summer of the first year of the war, with the sun taking the shape of a crescent and stars becoming visible. It was therefore a total solar eclipse.

The second solar eclipse took place in the eighth year of the war at the beginning of summer, although Thucydides only distinguishes two seasons here, summer and winter.

The lunar eclipse occurred in summer, eleven years after the second solar eclipse.

Detailed analyses of the official dating as well as two alternative dates can be found in Stephenson [Stephenson 1997, p. 346 ff.] and Fomenko [Fomenko 2003, vol. 1, p. 97 ff.], the latter also with references to previous research.

As Fomenko and other authors quite correctly state, the eclipse triad of the official history 431 BC => 424 BC => 413 BC cannot be correct if we take literally the statement about the first solar eclipse that "several stars appeared".

The degree of coverage of the sun during the eclipse over Greece was, at under 90 %, far too low for the visibility of stars or planets, even with correction of the delta-T value.

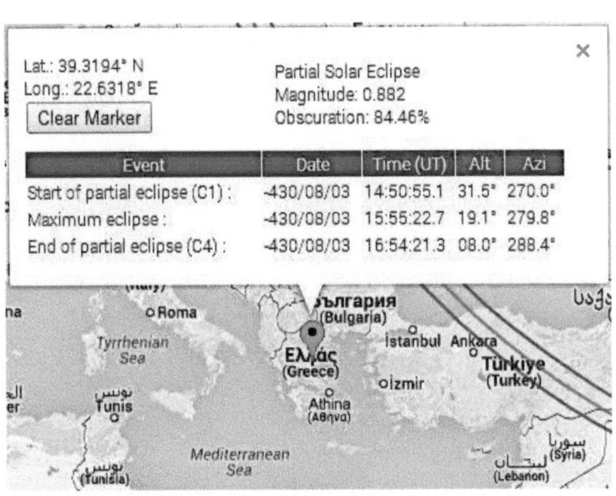

Fig. 97: The solar eclipse of Thucydides, traditionally 431 B.C., Source: http://eclipse.gsfc.nasa.gov

The only triad that is coherent with currently valid delta-T values was calculated by Morozov in 1928 [cited by Fomenko 2003, Vol. 1, p. 103 f.]. This lies almost exactly 3 x 521 years after the official dating in the years 1133 => 1140 => 1151.

Morozov's proposal, however, cannot convince for other reasons [see Arndt 2020/2, p.38]. Fomenko's proposal for the eclipse triad is 1039 => 1046 => 1057 [Fomenko 2003, vol. 1, p.103 ff]. He used a software for the calculation ("Turbo-Sky software") which gives different results than other authors and the NASA website, which is currently the reference for eclipse calculations [NASA]. Fomenko's proposal would only work if one assumes an even far larger delta-T anomaly than the official history. Therefore, Fomenko's proposal does not fit either.

The author's suggestion: If we ignore the scientifically unsubstantiated change in the delta-T value, an eclipse triad corresponding perfectly to the sources occurred in the years 693 => 700 => 711. The solar eclipse on 5 November 693 achieved an coverage of the sun of just under 100 % (crescent shape) in Greece, so that the brightest planets and stars were visible. To be precise, these were at least Venus and Sirius, possibly more.

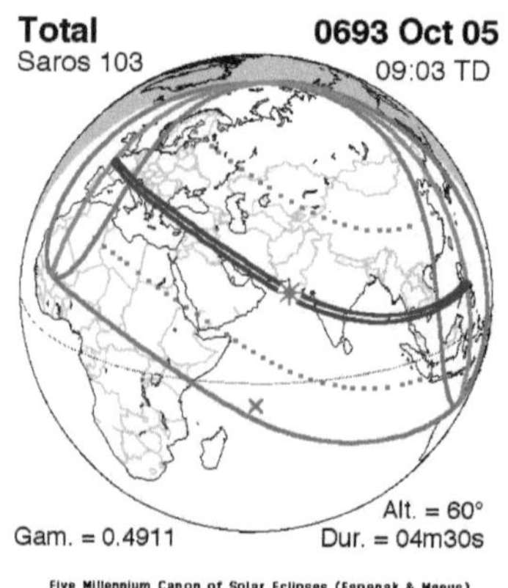

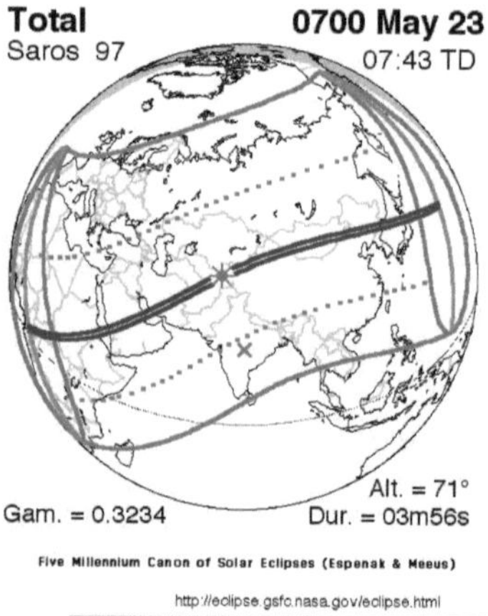

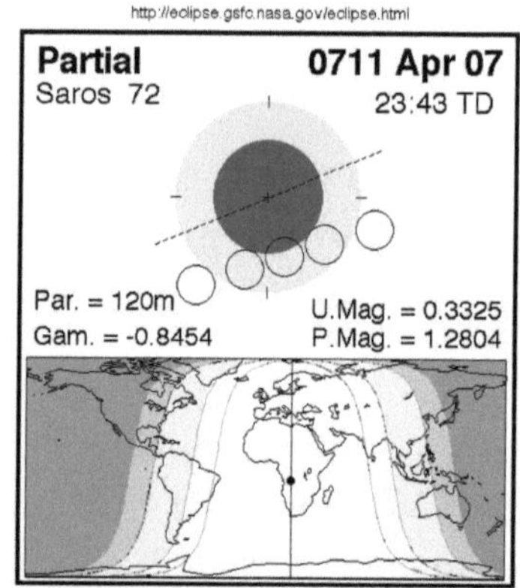

Fig. 98 (left): The solar eclipse of 5 October 693 (not 3 August 431 BC)

Fig. 99 (right): The solar eclipse of 23 May 700 (not 21 March 424 BC)

Fig. 100 (below): The lunar eclipse of 7 April 711 (not 27 August 413 BC)

A matching partial eclipse occurred seven years later on 23 May 700. And a matching lunar eclipse occurred on 7 April 711.

The difference between the author's dating and that of the official history is 1123 years. Later it will be shown that this time interval is correct for many other eclipse reports that come from written sources that are assigned to Greek antiquity.

For almost all eclipse reports of Greek antiquity a matching eclipse can be found if a difference of 1119-1123 years is assumed.

The problem with Delta T

The greatest uncertainty in eclipse calculations is due to changes in the Earth's rotation, mainly caused by the influence of the Moon. These variations in the Earth's rotation cause deviations of Universal Time from Terrestrial Time, called Delta T, which affect the visibility of calculated eclipses.

Universal Time is based on astronomical observation from Earth and therefore includes irregularities in the Earth's rotation. It is also the basis for official time.

To put it simply, Terrestrial Time is an ideal calculation value that excludes changes in the Earth's rotation. Terrestrial Time is therefore an absolutely uniform time scale. The practical realisation is achieved by use of atomic clocks.

Changes in the Earth's rotation have been very small in recent centuries with precise astronomical observations.

The calculations underlying the datings of official history now implicitly presuppose precisely the delta-T values with which there is an optimal matching between eclipse reports attributed to antiquity and the Middle Ages with back-calculations.

The unexpressed premise is that the chronology of official history is correct. Under this premise, however, very large delta-T values result for the distant past, in contrast to the last centuries, moreover with physical anomalies (see [Stephenson 1997] and [Morrison and Stephenson 2004]) as a basis for the NASA calculations.

Also important are Robert R. Newton's investigations of the Earth/Moon system and the elongation of the Moon [Newton 1970 and 1972].

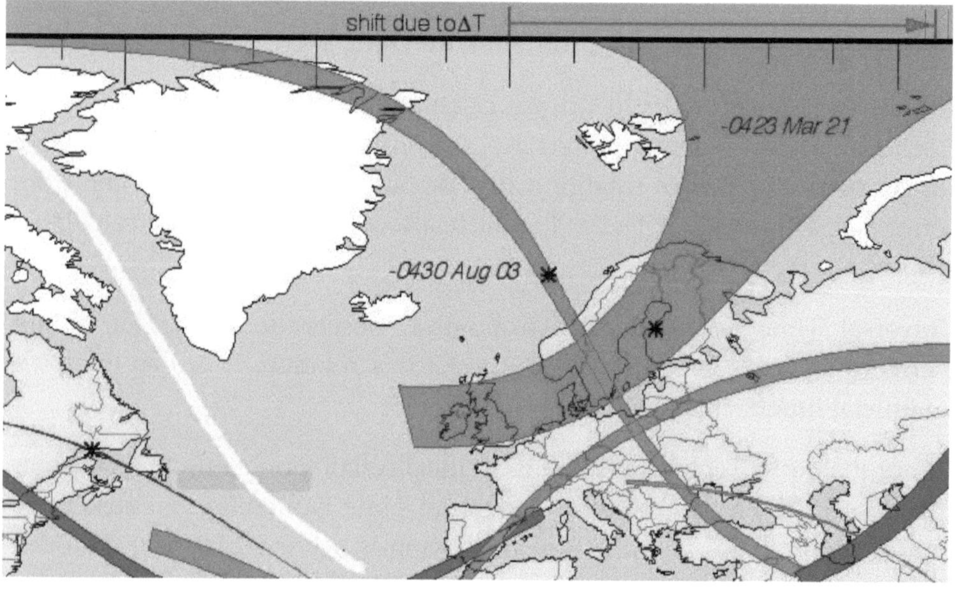

Fig. 101: The path of visibility of the annular solar eclipse 431 BC (and 424 BC) in Greece (according to Thucydides) according to official history in red, without delta-T correction bright (inserted by the author). The SoFi was therefore actually visible in the middle of the North Atlantic, but not at all in Greece (for details see pp. 140-142). The shift of the path due to the scientifically unsubstantiated delta-T change is fortunately noted at the top of the NASA map (original) (shift due to ΔT).
Source: http://eclipse.gsfc.nasa.gov

Even with this method, many but by no means all eclipse reports of antiquity can be linked to an actual recalculated eclipse. As the already quoted A. Demandt states, even with delta-T correction more than 80 % of all ancient eclipse reports do not match calculations [Demandt 1970].

Taking into account delta-T values for ancient times, which are also proven for later times, the path of the eclipses would be geographically shifted and the visibility would affect completely different regions. A change in the delta-T value by a certain amount would indeed move certain eclipses that are not observable now into the visibility range; but in doing so, the path of others shifts again in such a way that they are no longer (sufficiently) visible.

How do the delta-T values come about?

The British astronomer F. Richard Stephenson (* 1941) and his colleagues are responsible for the delta T values used in the NASA calculations (quasi the standard) [Stephenson 1997].

Fig. 102 (p. 152) shows the regions and dates for which written sources with observations of solar and lunar eclipses were used [see Stephenson 1997]. These are primarily

- Babylonian reports on cuneiform tablets from the time before 66 BC,
- Chinese reports from the period from the middle of the 5th century to about 700, 948 (one) and again from the middle of the 11th century,
- Arabic reports from the 9th century onwards.

In addition, there are some Greek reports that come from Ptolemy's "Almagest", as well as the only (!) solar eclipse of the entire Greco-Roman antiquity for which the exact observation time was written down.

This one comes from a commentary on Ptolemy's "Almagest" by Theon from Alexandria and describes the solar eclipse on 16 June 364 according to official history.

The historiography of Greco-Roman antiquity, which is usually so rich in detail, is strikingly absent. As has already been mentioned (see p. 146), not a single solar eclipse from ancient Europe has come down to us with details of the time of observation and other details.

In Mesopotamia, especially Babylon, the ability to write down precise observations of celestial events was cultivated, especially solar and lunar eclipses. It was the only region in the world at that time. Later, this became a practice in Egypt as well, passed down most notably in writings by the Greek Egyptian Claudius Ptolemy (c. 100-170 AD). Sometime after 66 BC, this ability was completely lost in Babylon, and somewhat later in Egypt.

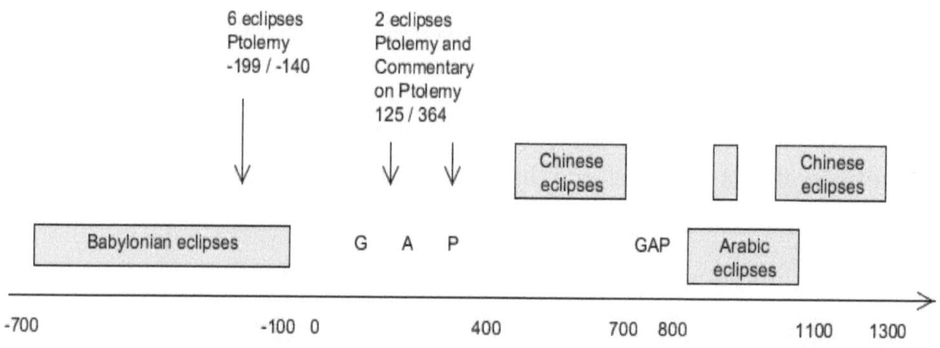

Fig. 102: The origin of the eclipse reports for NASA's delta-T values according to [Stephenson 1997, especially p. 504].

Almost 1000 years later, other people in the area of Babylon, in Baghdad, about 90 km away, had the idea of doing the same as their ancestors, who had long since disappeared along with the cuneiform tablets in the desert sand, and the Arabic eclipse reports began. In addition to Baghdad, the most important observation sites were Alexandria and Cairo (called "Babylon" in the Middle Ages) in Egypt, where it had also been possible to do this a few centuries earlier, but had then been forgotten again.

So here we are supposed to have a gap that lasted for many centuries in the exercise of skills that were quite unique at the time, which are now flourishing anew in the very places where they had been lost without trace centuries before. This is a pretty absurd notion.

Equally strange is the fact that until the 19th century, when these cuneiform tablets of the ancient Babylonians were found in the desert sands (and it was precisely from this time that it was only possible to make precise astronomical back-calculations to the time of ancient Babylon, but not yet quite as precise as today!), no one knew anything about these tablets. At that time, only Persian cuneiform tablets were known, and for a very long time.

Without these Babylonian eclipse reports, Greco-Roman antiquity has no firm anchor chronologically and cannot be clearly dated astronomically! This is true by today's standards of science, but not yet by those of Scaliger's time in the 16th/17th centuries.

Fig. 103: Cuneiform tablet, part of the Epic of Gilgamesh

The time between 66 BC (the last Babylonian eclipse considered by Stephenson) and 434 (the first Chinese eclipse) thus represents a rather enormous gap of 500 years. This period contains only two eclipses, which are also linked to the dubious Ptolemy, in the years 125 (lunar eclipse) and 364 (the already mentioned solar eclipse).

There is another large gap between 702 and 829, between Chinese and Arab eclipses. The last three of the Chinese eclipses around 700 date from the Tang dynasty (618-907), for which it has been proven that most of the surviving reports on eclipses can only be back-calculations and not actual observations [Stephenson 1997, p. 246]. Otherwise, the eclipses from China would have ended in 596 and the second gap of 233 years would have been much larger.

For more on Babylonian eclipses, see page 164.

The change of Delta T

The only source for delta-T values before the time with accurate observations by telescopes around 1600 AD are written reports of observations of solar and lunar eclipses in European, Middle Eastern and Chinese manuscripts.

In the period from about 1600 to the present, the delta T values are relatively small and also vary little over time. Before that, it was allegedly quite different - according to the evaluation of the reports on the premise that the official chronology is true. However, the methodology of determining the delta-T values is highly dubious [more details in Arndt 2020/2, p. 57/58]. E.g. for solar eclipse reports of the time around 1100, delta-T values between -1000 and 2900 seconds result (Fig. 104, p. 156). Everything is possible!

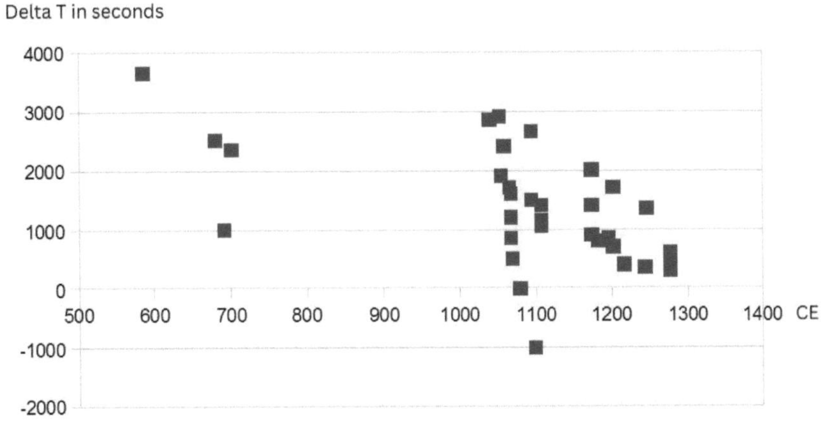

Fig. 104: Delta-T values derived from Chinese solar eclipses, according to [Stephenson 1997, p. 296/297].

It doesn't look much better at other times when there are a lot of observational values. Each one may decide for himself how significant individual high or low values (or any value at all) are with only a few eclipse reports or only one for several centuries, as is often the case with Stephenson's delta-T values with centuries-long gaps.

But the answer is obvious. The results are not significant, which means that the relevance of the determined delta-T values over many centuries is zero.

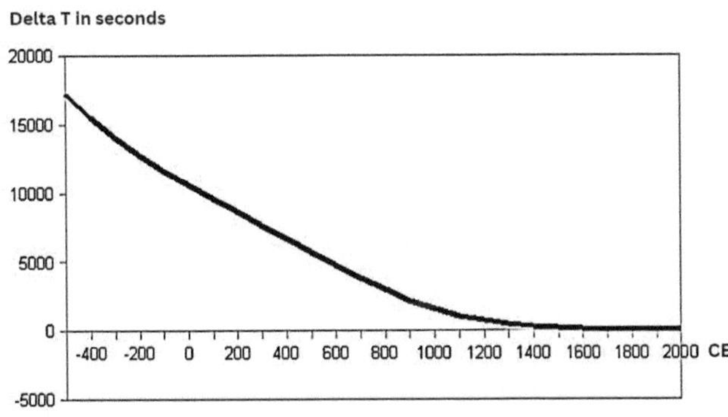

Fig. 105: The course of Delta T from 500 BC to the present. Delta T values derived from written sources. We can immediately see the completely different delta T values in the time before 1600 compared to the time after. Source: http://eclipse.gsfc.nasa.gov

This curve (or the equations describing it) is used in NASA's eclipse calculations, i.e. for any eclipses of the period in question. However, the delta-T correction is noted on overview maps (see e.g. Fig. 101).

This curve is therefore based exclusively on the eclipse reports that have been passed down (which are considered genuine without proof), their chronological classification according to official history and their scientifically questionable interpretation. It matches some of the eclipse reports, but by no means all of them.

I would now like to draw your attention to the analysis of the change in Delta-T. There are two remarkable points:

1) The change in delta T per century has practically the same value in the period 0-700 AD, deviating from the centuries before and after (see Fig. 106).

and most importantly:

2) For about the same period of about 700 years, the change in the change in delta T per century ("acceleration") decreases and not increases in the period from the beginning of the 5th century to about 1100 AD, unlike before and after (see Fig. 107).

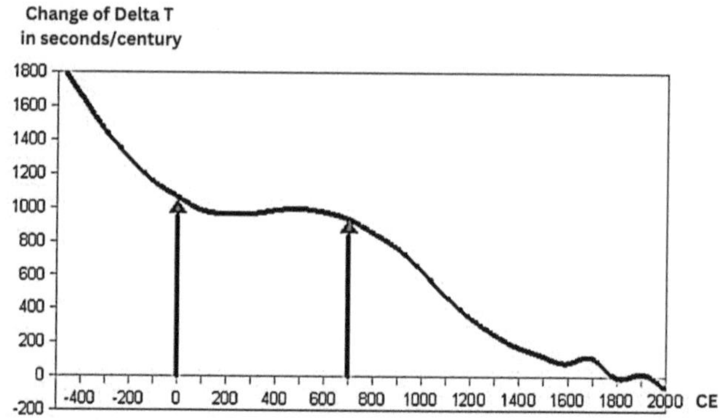

Fig. 106: The change of Delta T in seconds/century.
You can see inflection points at the beginning of our era and around 700.

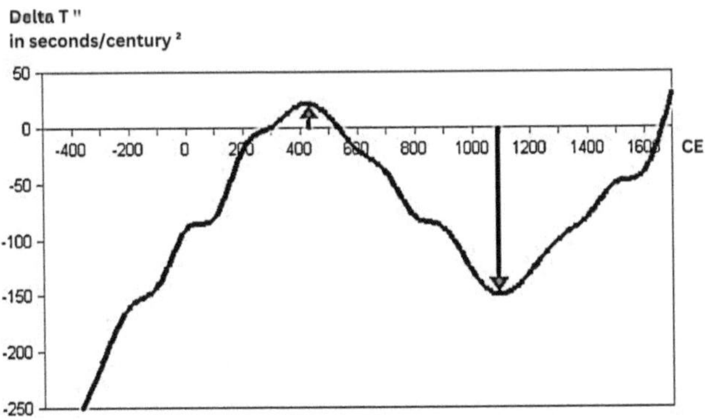

Fig. 107: The change in the change ("acceleration") of Delta T in seconds/ century². You can see inflection points in the 5th century and around 1100.

From this we can conclude that the reports of eclipses for the periods of

- before the beginning of the Christian era and afterwards,
- the time before and after about 700, and
- of the 5th - 11th century A.D., and before and after that

have originated differently. That this is indeed largely the case in a geographical sense, I have shown above with the analysis of the origin of the eclipse reports (see Fig. 102, p. 153). However, this is not sufficient to explain these anomalies.

Of course, the inflection points also correspond approximately to the inflection points in Robert R. Newton's curve of D'' of the elongation of the moon, since the sources for this are largely identical: the eclipse reports [Newton 1970 and 1972]. Newton cannot avoid concluding that hitherto unknown forces are at work.

Unzicker is probably not the only physicist who assumes here "an anomaly in the gravitational constant or even in the course of time" [Unzicker 2010, p. 82].

He is certainly right about the latter. However, it is not a question of physical time, but of the chronology constructed by man.

There are three alternatives:

1. there are up to now unknown physical forces that have led to the anomalies,
2. today's laws of physics did not apply in the distant past,
3. the chronology of the official history is wrong and 1. and 2. do not apply.

My proposal in this regard for the chronological classification of the passed down eclipse reports, which follows this chapter, is based on alternative 3. All other suggestions made so far, e.g. by the official history or also by some alternative authors, assume alternative 1 or 2.

The re-dating of the eclipses

The re-dating of the eclipses avoids the arbitrary assumption of scientifically unsubstantiated changes in the delta-T value in the course of the past. The author assumes that the delta-T values of the distant past in antiquity and the Middle Ages fluctuate only to about the same small extent as in the last centuries of precise astronomical observations. Indeed, there is no apparent reason to assume otherwise.

In this way, the anomalies that only arise from the incorrect assignment of the eclipse reports, which is a consequence of the incorrect chronology, disappear. There are constant differences of the eclipses to the official solution as follows:

a) Ancient Greek eclipses: 1120-1123 years

b) Ancient Roman eclipses until the end of the 4th century: 781 years

c) Eclipses from the 5th - 6th century: 521 years.

In addition:

d) Eclipses of Ptolemy: 1142 years (see ancient Greek eclipses)

e) Babylonian eclipses (cuneiform tablets): 1135 years, exceptions up to 1121 years (see ancient Greek eclipses)

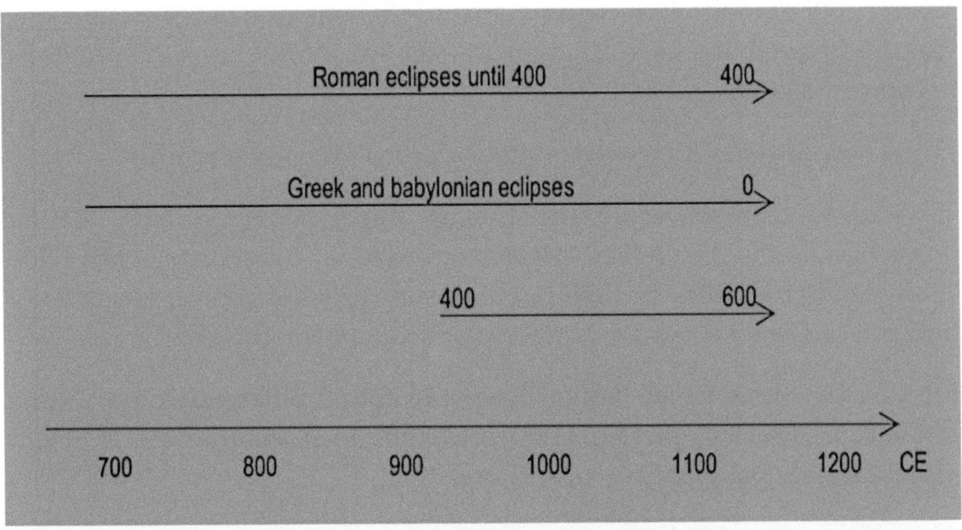

Fig. 108: The schematic classification of the eclipses in the chronology. At the very bottom, the timeline shows our chronology. The upper arrows are labelled with the years currently assigned to the corresponding eclipses according to official history.

There are astonishing matches in this assignment of the eclipses:

1.) The reliable Arab eclipse reports date from the 9th-11th centuries AD, and thus begin shortly before the eclipse reports of China and Europe, which according to official history are assigned to the period from the 5th century onwards (in Fig. 108 the arrow "400-600").

2.) The Babylonian eclipse reports, which have come down to us on cuneiform tablets, are also mainly in the same period, according to official history in the first pre-Christian centuries.

3.) The Roman eclipse reports, which today are wrongly dated before the end of the 4th century, also fall into the same period.

4.) Precisely from the 12th century onwards, a large number of reliable medieval eclipse reports have also been passed down from Europe, in contrast to before [Stephenson 1997].

Let us now turn to the concrete re-dating of the individual eclipses.

The Greek eclipses before the Roman imperial period have similar differences as the Babylonian eclipses recorded on cuneiform tablets (1135 years, see [Arndt 2012 p. 128ff.]). Greek history is, of course, inextricably linked with Oriental history. More on the Babylonian eclipses later.

Most of the author's new datings have a temporal difference to the dating of the official history of 1121-1123 years. Individual eclipses are 1119 and 1136 years (see Babylonian eclipses) later.

Already on pages 147 ff. the three eclipse reports of Thucydides during the Peloponnesian War were discussed in detail. For these, the author was able to find alternative solutions to the dating of official history at a time interval of 1123 years - in the years 693 => 700 => 711 AD.

Roman eclipses show a constant difference of about 781 years until the end of the 4th century (of which 781 years: 12, 780 years: 2, 779 years: 1, 783 years: 1).

For the recorded solar eclipses, where an exact day was given, there is an additional difference of 5-7 days, which needs explanation. 6 days is the difference of the spring equinox in 781 years. 7 days could be skipped without changing the day of the week, leaving only 3 days instead of 10 for the Gregorian calendar reform (1582) (corresponding to the shift of the spring equinox from the 12th to the 16th century).

From the beginning of the 5th century, a large number of eclipses exact to the day have been passed down to us (and at the same time in China and in Europe!), which had been very rare before - an astonishing, hitherto completely unexplained leap in the quality of the sources. The eclipses of Ptolemy were an exception, but only lunar eclipses are recorded, and surprisingly not a single solar eclipse.

Report	Event, Eclipse of the	Dating	Back calculation	New dating	Difference in years
Pliny et al. (Thales)	Sun	-583	28/5/ -584	20/6/ 540	1123
Thucydides	Sun	-430	3/8/ -430	5/10/ 693	1123
Thucydides	Sun	-423	21/3/ -421	23/5/ 700	1123
Thucydides	Moon	-412	27/8/ -412	7/4/ 711	1123
Xenophon	Moon	-405/04?	15/4/ -405	13/1/ 716	1121
Xenophon	Sun	-404/03?	3/9/ -403	3/6/ 718	1121
Xenophon	Sun	-394/93	14/8/ -393	8/1/ 726	1119
Diodor	Sun	-363	13/7/ -363	15/8/ 760	1123
Arrian, Plutarch et al. (Battle of Alexander - there is also a Babylonian cuneiform tablet)	Moon	20.-21/9/ -330	20.-21/9/ -330	21/9/ 796 or 1/9/ 806	1126 1136
Diodor	Sun	-309/308	15/8/ -309	14/5/ 812	1121
D. Laertios	Moon	-128	5/11/ -128	30/1/ 994	1122

Tab. 13: Greek eclipses of antiquity according to [Starke 2013, p. 251 ff.] with new datings, Partially two alternatives are available. Back calculations according to http://eclipse.gsfc.nasa.gov

The three eclipses of Thucydides have already been discussed on pages 147 ff.

Report	Event, Eclipse of the	Dating	Back calculation	New dating	Difference in years
Cicero	Moon	-62	3/5/ -62	2/11/ 719	781
C. Dio	Sun	5	28/3/ 5	3/4/ 786	781
Phlegon	Sun	32/33	14/11/ 29	30/11/ 810	781
C. Dio	Sun	1/8/ 45	1/8/ 45	7/8/ 826	781 + 6 days
A.Victor	Moon	47	1/1/ 47	6/1/ 828	781
Pliny	Sun	30/4/ 59	30/4/ 59	5/5/ 840	781 + 5 days
Pliny	Sun + Moon	71; interval of 15 days	4/3/ 71 20/3/ 71	9/3/ 852 24/3/ 852	781
Fast. Vind.	Sun	118	3/9/ 118	23/1/ 901	783
C. Dio	Sun	218-222	7/10/ 218	7/4/ 1000	781
Hist. Aug.	Sun	240	5/8/ 240	11/8/ 1021	781
Cons. Const.	Sun	291?	4/5/ 292	24/11/ 1071	780
A. Victor	Sun	317	6/7/ 316	25/12/ 1098	781
Cons. Const.	Sun	319	6/5/ 319	25/12/ 1098	779
Pappus	Sun	18/10/ 320	18/10/ 320	26/10/ 1147	827 + 8 days
F. Maternus	Sun	334	17/7/ 334	23/7/ 1115	781
A. Marcellinus	Sun	360	28/8/ 360	20/3/ 1140	780
Theon	Sun	16/6/364	16/6/ 364	23/6/ 1191	827 + 7 days
Fasti Vind.	Sun	26.-27/10/ 393	20/11/ 393	26/11/ 1174	781
Zosimus	Sun	5.-6/9/ 394	20/11/ 393	13/9/ 1178	784 + 7 days

Tab. 14: Roman eclipses of antiquity according to [Starke 2013, p. 251 ff.] until the end of the 4th century with new dating. In the case of the combination of solar eclipse + lunar eclipse by Pliny, the author's new dating actually results in an interval of 15 days according to the written source, which is not the case with the dating of the official history. In addition, the solar eclipse of Zosimus (Battle of Frigidus) is also listed. Back calculations according to http://eclipse.gsfc.nasa.gov

Report	Event, Eclipse of the	Dating	Back calculation	New dating	Difference in years
Hydatius et al.	Sun	11/11/ 402	11/11/ 402	11/11/ 923	521
Hydatius et al.	Sun	19/7/ 418	19/7/ 418	19/7/ 939	521
Hydatius et al.	Sun	23/12/ 447	23/12/ 447	22/12/ 968	521
Hydatius et al.	Moon	26/9/ 451	26/9/ 451	25/9/ 972	521
Hydatius et al.	Sun	28/5/ 458	28/5/ 458	28/5/ 979	521
Hydatius et al.	Moon (not Sun)	2/3/ 462	2/3/ 462	2/3/ 983	521
Hydatius et al.	Sun	20/7/ 464	20/7/ 464	20/7/ 985	521
M. Neapolit.	Sun	13-23/1/ 484	14/1/ 484	24/1/ 1004	520
Marcellinus	Sun	497	18/4/ 497	18/4/ 1018	521
Marcellinus	Sun	512	29/6/ 512	29/6/ 1033	521
Beda et al.	Sun	14/2/ 538	15/2/ 538	15/2/ 1059	521
Beda et al.	Sun	20/6/ 540	20/6/ 540	20/6/ 1061	521
Gregory et al.	Sun	1/10/ 563	3/10/ 563	2/10/ 1084 (Degree of coverage is correct)	521
Gregory et al.	Sun, or Moon?	mid-October 590	4/10/ 590	Moon 18/10/ 1111 (Mid Oct. is right)	521

Tab. 15: Eclipses of the 5th - 6th century [according to Starke, p. 251 ff.] with new datings.

The eclipse on 2 March 462 was not, as Starke writes, a solar eclipse, but a lunar eclipse. Text of the written source "ab occasu solis luna in sanguinem plena conuertitur ". This took place on 2 March 983.

In the author's alternative dating of the SoFi 2 October 1084, the degree of coverage of about 80 % in Tours agrees with the statement in the source "that only about a quarter of its surface was visible". This is not the case with the dating of the official story 3 October 563 (well below 50 %).

The eclipse in mid-October 590/ 18 October 1111 was obviously a lunar eclipse, and not a solar eclipse, according to the author. Thus the source specification "mid-October" is also correct, which is not the case according to official history (4 October). This lunar eclipse is also reported by Fredegar.

Babylonian eclipses

The ancient Babylonians had not yet discovered America, but they calculated, among other things, partial lunar eclipses with a degree of coverage of less than 50%, which were only visible in America (as well as on the shores of the Pacific), but not in Mesopotamia, e.g. that of 9 April 731 BC. This is what official history claims in all seriousness.

Fig. 109: The Tower of Babel, Painting by Pieter Bruegel (1563)

But calculating partial lunar eclipses for observers in America was not enough for them.

No, they also chiselled their calculations into cuneiform tablets that had been buried in the desert sands for thousands of years!

Surprisingly, Babylon was much more precise with its records of celestial observations 1000 years before other parts of the world, and they also largely correspond to today's back-calculations.

The cuneiform tablets, on which, among other things, celestial observations were documented, were found in the second half of the 19th century . The translation of the cuneiform tablets, some of which were quite simple, was carried out in cooperation with historians, linguists and astronomers. In the process, for example, it was first defined which word was to be used for which celestial body or constellation.

Since there was of course no doubt at all about the validity of the official chronology, it was also clear which planets or constellations could be expected and which could not. There are also enough gaps and missing fragments.

Back-calculation of solar eclipses was easily possible at the time of discovery and translation in the mid/late 19th century. In 1887, as is well known, Oppolzer's famous "Canon der Finsternisse" (Canon of Eclipses) was published. Therefore, it is possible that the vocabulary created for astronomy was already preformed by expectations, and thus they only reproduced what they expected to see in the sky.

By the way, after the great shopping tour of European museums in Mesopotamia at the end of the 19th century (whereby the archaeological context is often unclear), not a single clay tablet with astronomical content was found.

But: In contrast to the clay tablets, the coins of that time have been inscribed in Greek since Alexander the Great (336 - 323 B.C.) until the end of the Arsakid dynasty (Parthian Empire) in 224 A.D. Therefore, what are completely Babylonian cuneiform tablets without Greek or Aramaic texts supposed to mean in this period?

Without these cuneiform tablets, an astronomical assignment of the early medieval and ancient eclipses from Europe that is halfway scientifically substantiated by today's standards would not be possible at all.

The credibility of the chronology of Roman-Greek antiquity, which Scaliger in the 16th century had classified in this way with the help of astronomy, depends decisively on these Babylonian cuneiform tablets, since there is not a single European eclipse of this time that can be reliably dated astronomically (no precise descriptions of the eclipse observations available).

The Babylonian eclipses are quasi the lifeline without which Roman-Greek antiquity would be completely free-floating in the time axis from an astronomical-chronological point of view - by today's standards, but not yet by Scaliger's standards in the 16th century.

The author has found the actual solar eclipses for all Babylonian eclipse reports to be 1135 years later (700 + 435) (usually: 1135 or 1132/33, exceptions to -14 years). 435 years is the time difference between the Seleucid era (-311) and the Nabonasser era (-746) introduced by Claudius Ptolemy but never used by the Babylonians, which may have been confused here, so that this difference could have come about.

Since some reports of solar eclipses are linked to planetary observations, a different assignment of planetary names was made [Arndt 2020/2, p. 194 ff].

The path of the widely discussed Babylonian solar eclipse of 136 BC [Hunger and Sachs, Schmidt] on the surface of the Earth does not actually run over Babylon at all, but over central and south-western Europe. It was easily observable on Mallorca in Spain, for example.

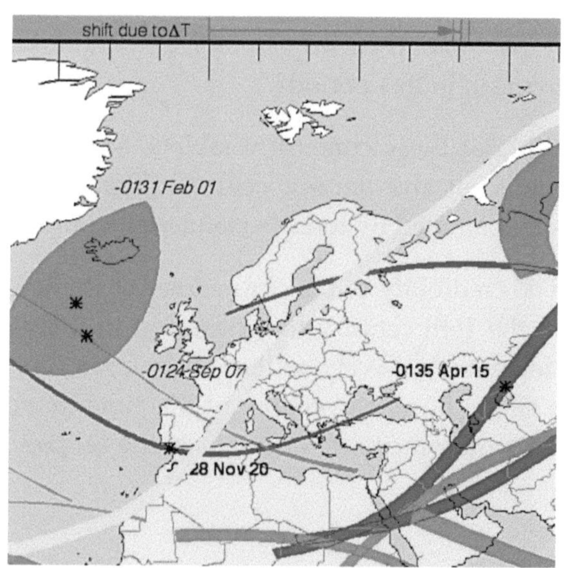

Fig. 110: The path of visibility of the solar eclipse on 15 April 136 BC (-135) with delta-T correction in blue (see (shift due to ΔT above), and bright without delta-T correction (inserted by the author). The eclipse was therefore actually visible in central and south-western Europe, but not at all in Babylon.
Source: http://eclipse.gsfc.nasa.gov

Only through the arbitrary assumption of physical anomalies in the distant past and a corresponding correction of the delta-T value does the path of the solar eclipse run thousands of kilometres further east and over Babylon.

With a difference of 1135 years minus 8 days, the eclipse is in the year 1000, on 7 April.

At current Delta-T, this eclipse has over 80% coverage in Babylon. With a normalisation of delta-T, it lands a few degrees further west, so that it is total in Babylon.

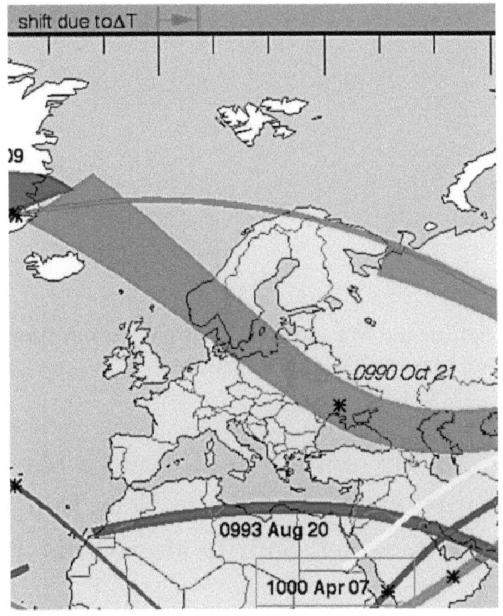

Fig. 111: The path of visibility of the solar eclipse on 7 April 1000 with delta-T correction in blue (see (shift due to ΔT above), and bright without delta-T correction (added by the author). The eclipse was therefore a total solar eclipse in Babylon.

Reports on this solar eclipse are available on two cuneiform tablets. Furthermore, one of the cuneiform tablets also describes a lunar eclipse in the same month, as well as planetary observations four days before the solar eclipse and immediately afterwards.

Following the translation of the first report according to the official history, the planets Venus, Mercury, Jupiter and Mars were visible during the solar eclipse.

Considering the alternative assignment of the planet names, the following were actually visible: Venus (= Venus), Saturn (= Mercury), Mercury (= Jupiter) and Mars (= Mars) (see Fig. 112).

Fig. 112: The visibility of the planets Mercury, Venus, Saturn and Mars as well as bright stars during the total solar eclipse on 7 April 1000. Jupiter had just set. Mars rose shortly afterwards.

Immediately after the solar eclipse, the following night, there follows a planetary observation concerning Venus. Venus was right next to Beta Tauri (constellation Taurus), as described on the clay tablet. Shortly afterwards it had reached the stationary point.

Four days earlier, a planet was standing right next to Alpha Tauri (constellation Taurus), but not Mercury, as previously translated, but Saturn.

A little more than two weeks before the solar eclipse, on 22 March, there was a lunar eclipse. The position of the moon is practically identical to that of 136 BC in the constellation Virgo. At the time of the lunar eclipse, the moon was therefore under the star Gamma Virginis (constellation Virgo). This matches well with today's retrocalculations (see Fig. 113-115).

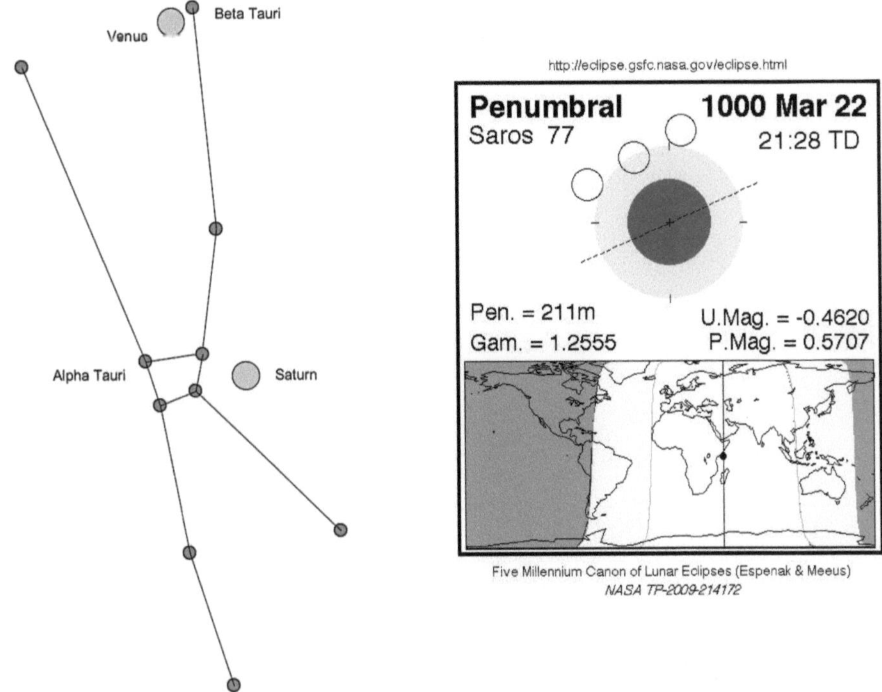

Fig. 113 (top right): The lunar eclipse of 22 March 1000, shortly before the solar eclipse of 7 April 1000.

Fig. 114 (top left): The constellation Taurus with Venus directly next to Beta Tauri on 7 April 1000 and Saturn next to Alpha Tauri four days earlier. Venus is approximately in the same position as it was on 15 April -135, and Saturn is approximately where Mercury was 1135 years earlier.

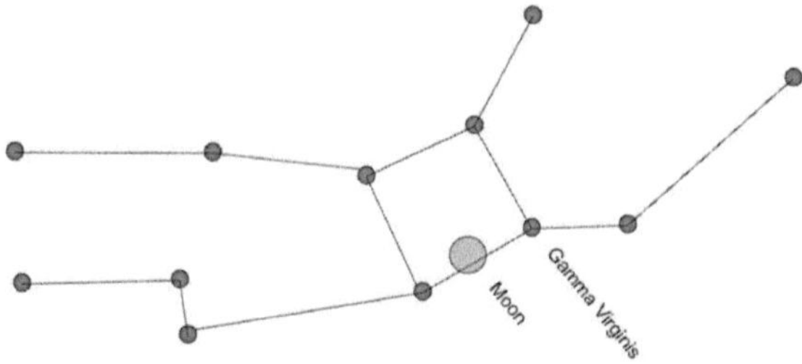

Fig. 115: The constellation of Virgo with the Moon under Gamma Virginis at the time of the lunar eclipse on 22 March 1000.

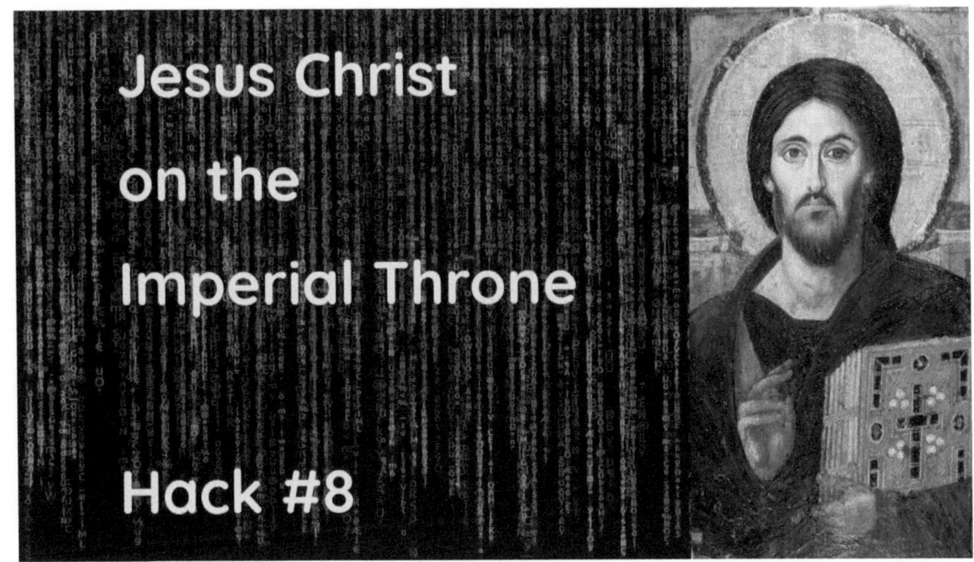

Introduction

With the help of astronomy, the author is now able to present a model that shows a different chronology, where the match with the written sources is practically as good as with the official chronology, in some cases even better (see page 159).

My model is more consistent with the history of science, as it places the ancient Greeks and Romans in the Middle Ages, along with the Arabs (e.g. Alexander the Great becomes king: 801 AD, death: 814 AD, Seleucid era: 825 AD).

This makes it possible to create a chronology in which the continuity of development becomes visible and the strange breaks and gaps in official history disappear or find a simple explanation.

I oppose the bumpiness of official history and catastrophism with the idea of continuity.

Let us now move on to today's Christian counting of years, as this is nowadays widespread worldwide and familiar to everyone. The starting point is the time of the assumed birth of the founder of Christianity, Jesus Christ, which was fixed in the Middle Ages.

Francesco Carrotta had already identified a Roman emperor as the model for Jesus Christ: Julius Caesar. Anatoli Fomeno claimed, that Jesus Christ lived in the 12th century, as Byzantine emperor Andronikos II.

But what really happened about 2020 years ago? Can it still be reconstructed today?

Jesus from the Old Testament at the beginning of our era

Easter is the most important feast in Christianity. It celebrates the resurrection of Jesus Christ after his death on the cross. Easter can be traced back to the Exodus of the people of Israel from Egypt and their salvation from slavery.

On the evening before the Exodus, on the 14th of Nisan in the Jewish calendar (identical with the first full moon after the beginning of spring), at God's command, the doorposts of the houses where the Jewish Passover festival was celebrated were to be smeared with the blood of the sacrificed lambs so that their inhabitants could be saved.

Jesus Christ was also crucified on the 14th of Nisan, a Friday, according to the Gospel of John, at the time of the sacrifice of the Passover lambs. The "Lamb of God" is a common symbol of Jesus Christ in Christianity.

According to official history, the counting of years "from Anno Incarnatione Domini" (since the Incarnation of the Lord) is supposed to correspond to another counting of years available in sources, the "Anno Salutis" year. Both calendars are therefore supposed to be at the beginning of our present Christian era.

This calendar era "Anno Salutis" clearly refers to a salvation event. Since "Salus" means "salvation, healing, health", it can only refer to the salvation of the people of Israel from their slavery during the exodus from Egypt.

"This is a day to remember. Each year, from generation to generation, you must celebrate it as a special festival to the LORD. This is a law for all time."
(Exodus 12,14)

In the same year God revealed the Ten Commandments. The year 2448 according to the Jewish calendar (starting from 3761 BC, cf. last chapter) is the year 1312/1313 BC, the year in which, mythically transfigured according to the Old Testament, Moses climbed Mount Sinai to receive the Tablets of the Law from God Himself.

"And for forty days and forty nights Moses was there with the Lord. (...) And he put in writing on the stones the words of the agreement, the ten rules of the law."
(Exodus 34,28)

Fig. 116: Jesus from the Old Testament - called "Joshua" according to the Vulgate version of the Bible, now chronologically 1313 years before the New Testament Jesus.

A noble beginning for the start of a new era. Thus Yom Kippur, the most important Jewish holiday on the 10th day of the new Jewish year, is a reminder of the end of the 40 days that Moses spent on Mount Sinai and God made the covenant with the people.

Another figure from the Old Testament has the same name as the Jesus of the New Testament. The most important army leader of the Old Testament (Book of "Jesus"/in Latin from Vulgate: Book of "Joshua") was Jesus. As a contemporary and immediate successor of Moses, he led the people of Israel into the Holy Land, defeated all the nations there, conquered the land and distributed it to the tribes.

This person is still called "Jesus" (Iησους) in Greek, Church Slavonic as well as Russian. Only in Latin (from Vulgate onwards) and the Bible translations based on it is this person called "Joshua" in order to distinguish him from the newly created New Testament figure "Jesus".

The Koran does not know a time gap of 1313 years between the Exodus from Egypt and the birth of Jesus Christ. In the Koran, Jesus is called "Isa" (On a fresco in the monastery of Hosios Lukas in Greece, the Old Testament Jesus is called "ICO" = Iso, see Fig. 116).

Isa belongs to the time of Moses. He is born as the son of Moses' sister, Mary/Miriam, and is supposed to kill the Antichrist and his followers before the end of the world after his return to earth. In Islam, Jesus is not "sacrificed", i.e. crucified, but raised directly by God to heaven. [Tabari p. 114]

The name Christ (from the Greek Χϱιστός = the anointed one) is nothing other than a reference to his kingship. In biblical Israel, the elevation to king was effected by means of ritual anointing by the highest priest. Christians are thus nothing other than followers of the king, in contrast to followers of other rulers or his enemies.

This also allows us to explain more convincingly why the Christian symbol was the fish (especially as a secret symbol among the "early Christians").

The Old Testament Jesus is repeatedly described as the "Son of Nun". But "Nun" is actually just the Aramaic word for "fish".

So from when do people officially count the years since Christ's birth? The documents of the Roman Catholic Church (in a sense of its representative) are dated by incarnation years only from the late 14th century onwards. In the Roman-Byzantine Empire, that is, where Christianity originally came from, years were never counted after Jesus Christ until the end (1453). In the third Rome, the Moscow Empire, it was not until 1700 AD that the calendar was changed from the creation of the world to the birth of Jesus Christ.

It is therefore surprising that we have a number of royal charters with dates according to the Christian calendar that date from the time of Charlemagne, his successors and the kings of the East Frankish/Roman-German Empire. Less surprising in this context would be that all these documents would be forgeries from later times, at least into the 13th century. As already mentioned at the beginning, according to H.C. Faußner, from a legal-historical point of view, almost all royal charters before 1122 (Worms Concordat) are in fact forgeries [Faußner 2003].

What about the connection of the counting of years since the foundation of the city of Rome with the Christian calendar? It was only determined late on which year from urbe condita (foundation of Rome) the year 1 AD corresponds. Dionysius Exiguus does not yet make this connection. Generally, the time around 600 and Pope Boniface IV are mentioned here.

Since this time, the equation for converting the era since the founding of the city of Rome (ab urbe condita) to the era after the birth of Christ (Anno Domini) has been valid:

754 a.u.c = 1 AD, i.e. the foundation of Rome was in 753 BC.

Fig. 117: Jesus Christ as warrior

The author has shown in [Arndt 2010], based on the 12th century chronicle of Lupus Protospatharius Barensis, that due to a different foundation date of Rome, the year 1 AD was originally in the 11th century. This chronicler sees the foundation of Rome (ab urbe condita) after the beginning of the Anno Salutis year count, namely in the year 258 Anno Salutis.

According to prevailing opinion, the Anno Salutis year count should be the same as the Anno Domini year count, i.e. our present-day Christian calendar. Then the foundation of Rome in today's chronology would be 1011 years before the foundation of Rome in the chronicle of Lupus.

If we now take the year 258 Anno Salutis according to Lupus as the basis for the foundation of Rome, then the year 1012 (258 + 754) of our present-day chronology results for the year 1 AD.

So today's Christian calendar obviously originally had a different reference point, namely the Exodus from Egypt, today dated to 1313 BC - with the connection to Jesus from the Old Testament described above. By converting the dates for the founding of Rome to values valid today, we find that the life of Jesus Christ was shifted 1010-1011 years into the past, just as the date of the founding of Rome was (see Fig on p. 177).

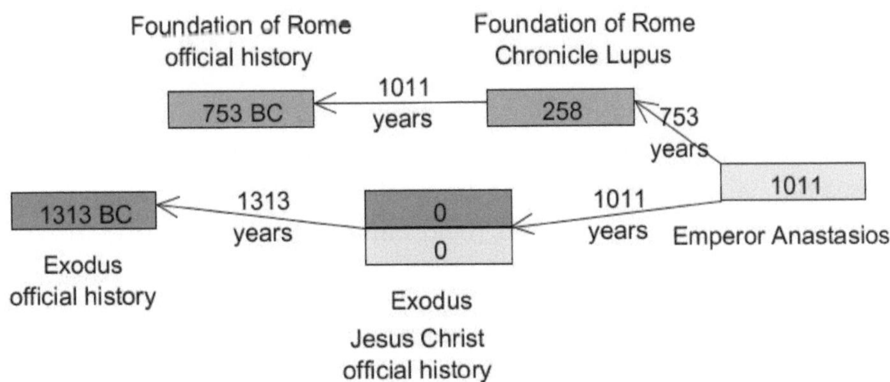

The Resurrected One on the Emperor's Throne

At this point, a brief reference to quite obviously faked approx. 300 years of Roman history between Emperor Constantine I (306-337) and Emperor Phocas (602-610) is necessary. After all, since the rise to power of Constantine I, who used to be considered the first Christian emperor, not a single emperor had been assassinated by (or on behalf of) his successor on the throne until the putsch of Phocas.

Almost all emperors between 337 and 602 died of natural causes, only a few in a battle against external enemies. But not a single emperor was assassinated, as was the rule rather than the exception before 337 and from 602 onwards. Here, quite obviously, the already fabricated history has been strikingly embellished.

It is strikingly common to find namesakes of the emperors of the time before 602 in the time after 602. If the emperors died a natural death before 602, their namesakes were generally murdered from 602 onwards. In the case of these pairs of emperors, the biographies were obviously split up in order to fill made-up time in the chronology of official history. This also applies to emperors named Anastasios and Justinian, among others.

Anastasios I: 491-518, Anastasios II: 713-715/716, failed coup 719
Justinian I: 527-565, Justinian II: 685-695 and 705-711

In Hack #7 it was shown that reports of solar and lunar eclipses of the time between 400 and 600 AD match equally well and even better with actual eclipses 521 years later according to recalculation. Starting from 521 AD, this would mean for the year 491 (beginning of the reign of the Byzantine Emperor Anastasios I):

521 + 491 = 1012. The year 1012 corresponds to the first year of the Resurrected One, Jesus Christ, as described above.

Anastasios means " the Resurrected One" and is a synonym for Jesus Christ. According to official history, Anastasios consolidated the Roman Empire after the Crisis of the Empire in the 5th century - a true resurrection! Because of his coinage reform, in numismatics the Byzantine Empire usually begins with him.

Anastasios I was the last Roman emperor to hold the title of "Pontifex", a title also held by Roman Catholic popes. So after Anastasios, someone else had to take over this office.

After Anastasios I, no Roman emperor was called "Divus" (the Divine). This honouring of Roman rulers is said to date back to Julius Caesar. The worship as "Divine" is also connected with the Ascension, i.e. the Divine Anastasios enters the afterlife without dying.

According to tradition, there were end-time expectations at his time. The Second Coming of Jesus Christ is said to have been expected. Some saw Anastasios I as the Anti-Christ.

Fig. 119: Coin of the Ressurected One as warrior, Emperor Anastasios I (491-518)

His namesake Emperor Anastasios II was forced to resign in 715/716 and then lived in a monastery for three years. In 719 he wanted to overthrow the incumbent emperor Leo III. The attempt failed and Anastasios was executed.

Peter on the Emperor's Throne

His successor on the imperial throne was Justin I, who reigned only briefly. Afterwards, a certain Peter became emperor, under the name Justinian I. As emperor, he was also the highest church leader in the Roman state church, something like the popes later in the West, the first of whom was also called Peter.

Justinian I resolutely promoted Christianisation and vigorously persecuted non-Christians. He introduced compulsory baptism for all children in the Roman Empire (except for Jews), which meant that practically all those born in the Roman Empire became Christians (except the Jews). He also had Plato's Academy in Athens closed down, for example.

Fig. 120: Barberini diptych, depicting either Emperor Anastasios I or Justinian I

The brother of this Peter on the imperial throne was called Paul and was consul. Even today, a memorial day commemorates the two apostles and church fathers Peter, the successor of the Resurrected One, and Paul.

Thus, these names of early Christian history have probably been taken over from Eastern Roman history.

The namesake Justinian II was the first emperor to mint coins with the pictorial representation of Jesus Christ with the inscription "DN IHS CHS REX REGNANTIUM" = Our Lord Jesus Christ King of Kings (= Emperor). Like the second Anastasios, he too was overthrown and executed.

Fig. 121: Solidus of Emperor Justinian II (668-711) with the first portrait of Jesus Christ on a coin.

The Star of Bethlehem

Matthew's Gospel tells of a striking phenomenon in the sky that was visible at the time of the birth of Jesus Christ.

"After Jesus was born in Bethlehem in Judea, during the time of King Herod, Magi from the east came to Jerusalem and asked, "Where is the one who has been born king of the Jews? We saw his star when it rose and have come to worship him." … and the star they had seen when it rose went ahead of them until it stopped over the place where the child was." [Matthew 2,1]

It is an undecided question what kind of celestial phenomenon this "star" is. There are various theories, all of which assume the dating of the birth of Jesus Christ around the beginning of our era. Some think it is a comet or a nova, others think it is a conspicuous conjunction of Jupiter and Venus or Jupiter and Saturn.

When dating the appearance of the Risen Christ to the year 1012 (521 + 491), the accession of the Byzantine Emperor Anastasios I, a nova would be the answer.

Anastasios I became emperor on 11 April 491, the Wednesday before Easter Sunday.

The chronicles all report the eruption of a nova for the year 1012 (+/- 6 years) - obviously the "Star of Bethlehem".

"A new star had appeared in the sky in spring (two sources: week after Easter), which was said to have been visible next to the sun in the daytime sky for three months."
[E.G. Annales Sangallenses, quoted in Newton 1972, p. 106-107]

According to Newton, this part of the Annales Sangallenses has a consistent error of 6 years. Thus the year 1012 is quite correct, since the Annales Sangallenses give the year 1006.

Thietmar of Merseburg [quoted in Newton 1972, p. 108] gives the year 1013 for the "new star in the daytime sky", also after Easter.

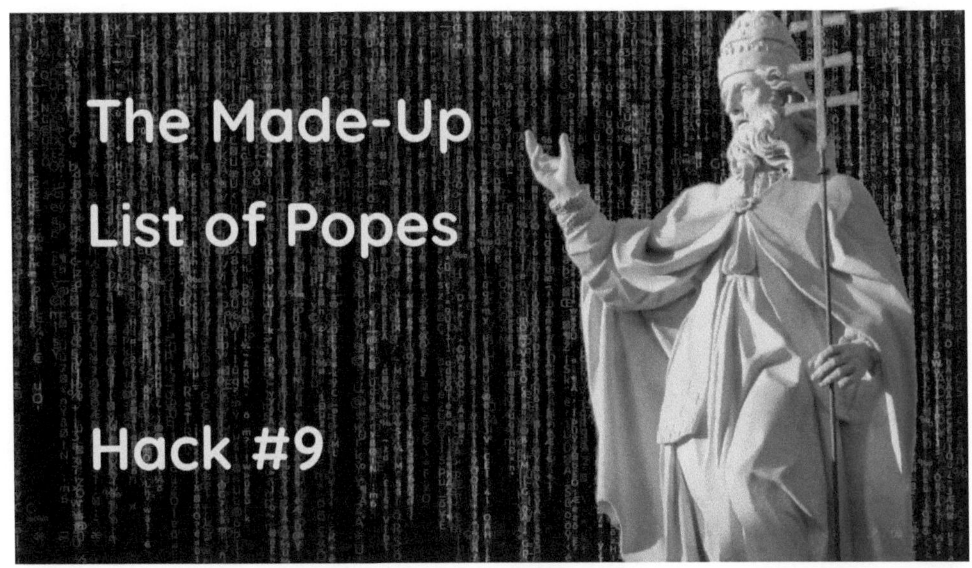

The made-up list of popes

In the media, one question distracts from the real issue: Was there a pope Joan?

As everyone knows, the supposedly powerful popes of the Middle Ages did not build impressive cathedrals like other bishops of that era.

So the crucial question is: Were there any popes at all in antiquity and in the Middle Ages?

Since the New Testament of the Bible is a literary fiction, many of the Roman Catholic popes in antiquity and in the Middle Ages are also ficticious.

Jesus Christ hands over the keys of the kingdom of heaven to Peter, his successor and first Pope of Rome - a fiction.

Fig. 122 : Christ handing the keys to Peter

And the following list of Roman Catholic popes is then of course also a fake. The author's analysis has revealed: At least the parts of the list of popes 141-314 and from 685-1455 (first Borgia Pope Callixt III) are quite obviously made up. These parts consist of

a) slightly altered copies of previous sections, and

b) constructions that follow certain algorithms.

E.g. the period from 384-530 serves as a template for a copy for the period from 687-891 regarding the tenures. The period from 523-685 serves as a template for a copy for the period from 685-858 regarding names.

In the period from 685-858 (173 years) there is a high correlation in terms of the names of the popes compared to 523-685 (162 years).

More precisely
1) identical names,
2) very similar names, or
3) an identical pattern of name repetition.

These characteristics apply to 50% of all the names of the popes of this period.

Some examples:

A slightly varied copy of the section from 523-608 with the popes Sylvester II and Sylvester III contains 14 popes from 984-1048. This section is structured around the popes Gregory V as the first German pope (counterpart: Boniface II as the first Germanic pope) and Clement II as the second German pope (counterpart: Pelagius II as the second Germanic pope). Both popes are separated by a period of 466 years. Note also the pairs Philagathos/Agapitos, Sylvester/Silverius, G. di Sabina/Sabinianus!

984	530
Boniface VII John XV	Boniface II **(= Gregor V 466 years apart)** John II
Gregory V (= Boniface II 466 years apart)	
John XVI Philagathos **Sylvester**	Agapitos **Silverius**
21 years	**24 years**
John XIX **Benedict IX**	John III **Benedict I**
Sylvester III (Giovanni di Sabina**)**	
Gregory VI **Clement II (466 years apart)**	**Pelagius II (466 years apart)** Gregory I Sabinianus

Table 16: Popes from 530 onwards and from 984 onwards in comparison, Copy of the list of popes from 530 in the years from 984, with the 1st and 2nd Gothic and German popes in parallel!

Another example in the made-up list of popes: The section from 844 - 911 is partly a construction (beginning and end) and partly a slightly varied copy of the section 1276-1334 beginning 418 years later, which is clearly constructed (as shown below). It contains 18 popes.

Note also the arrangement of the popes named Anastasius!

Popes 844 - 911	Popes 1276 - 1334	Difference
Sergius II Leo IV Benedict III		
Antipope Anastasius III		
Nicholas I **Hadrianus II** **John VIII**	**Hadrianus V** **John XXI** **Nicholas III**	418 years
Mar(t)inus I **Hadrianus III** (HDRNS) Stephen V Formosus Boniface VI Stephen Romanus Theodore John IX	**Martin II** **Honorius IV** (HNRS) Nikolaus IV Celestine V Boniface VIII Benedict XI Clement V --------------- John XXII	 418 years
Benedict IV Leo V Sergius III	Benedict XII	
Anastasius III		

Table 17: The well-structured list of popes from 844-911. A pope named Anastasius ("the resurrected one") follows in 911. (H)Adrianus/Honorius are arranged in parallel several times throughout the papal list. Popes with the name Theodore ("God's gift") are the only popes to stand several times without a parallel pope. Popes with the name Marinus were formerly listed as Martinus.

The boundaries in the years 384, 530, 687 and 891 correspond to the end of the respective versions of the "Liber pontificalis" (official "Book of the Popes") as they have been passed down through written sources and are thus historically well-founded. The fact that there are also breaks in the structuring precisely at these boundaries (and others) proves the artificial character of the entire list of popes.

The list of popes from 1046 onwards consists of constructions that follow certain algorithms. The copied or constructed sections each have a length of 10 (once), 14 (three times), 18 (three times) or 21 (once) popes.

The list of popes from 1046 -1145 (18 popes) is clearly fabricated (see right side). The popes numbered "II" are dominant, at the beginning still alternated with "IX". Exactly in the middle are two popes with different numbering.

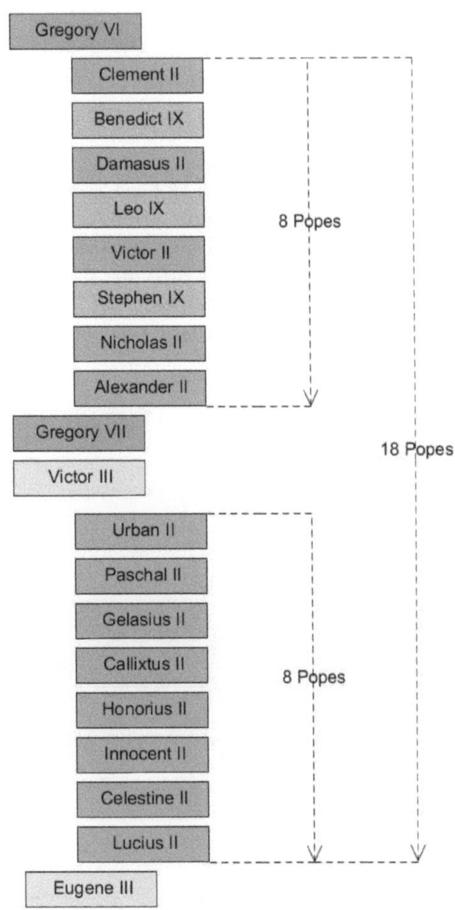

From 1145 - 1276 there are also 18 popes (see right side), at the beginning and at the end a pope with the name Adrian. The popes with the numbers "III" and "IV" are dominant one after the other, at the end "V". This pattern is only interrupted by popes with the name "Gregory", as also from 1046 – 1145 (see p. 187).

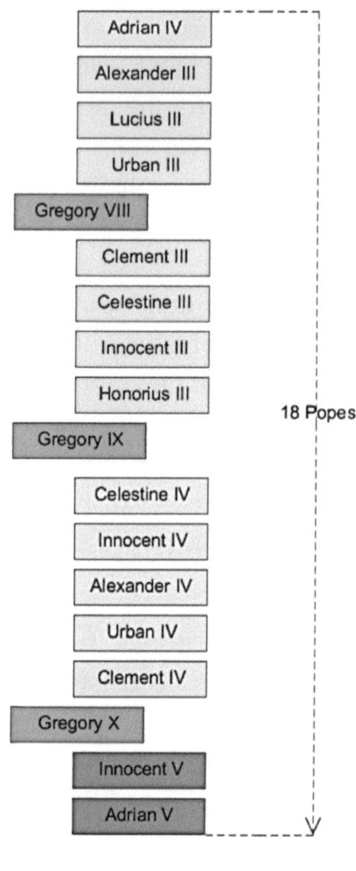

Fig. 125 (below): The arrival of Pope Gregory XI in Rome in 1377 (fresco by Giorgio Vasari, ca. 1571-1574). From 1309 to 1377, Avignon in France was the seat of the Pope. It is also only since this time that the Pope's list loses its artificial character (on this, see the author's book "The Well-Structured History" [in German])

The list from 1277 - 1455 (see p. 189) begins and ends with a Pope Nicholas (before the first Borgia Pope Callixt III).

A clearly visible construction, but somewhat more complicated. Immediately visible are the beginning and the end (Martin -> Nicholas) and the popes around John XXII, the first pope to begin his pontificate in Avignon.

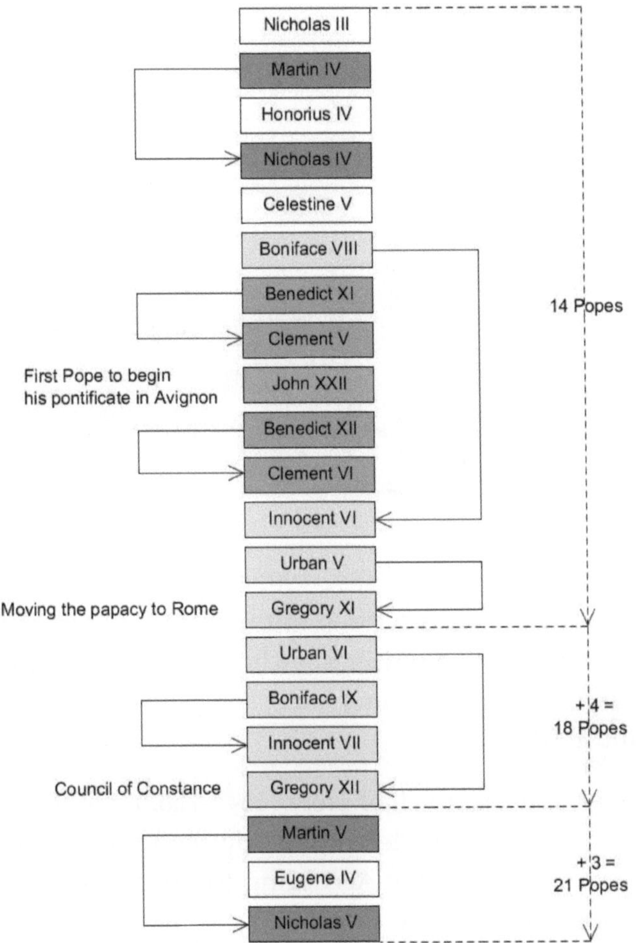

The Borgia and Medici popes of the 15th/16th century are doubled as Counts of Tusculum, who became popes in the 10th/11th century. Their pontificates were (almost) exactly 500 years before.

John XII (955-964)	Callixtus III (1455-1458)
Sylvester II (999-1003), who is not Count of Tusculum. Sylvester II lived for a long time in (at that time) Aragon, the country of origin of the Borgias, where he received his education and studied.	Alexander VI (1492-1503)
Benedict VIII (1012-1024)	Leo X. (1513-1523)
John XIX (1024-1032)	Clement VII (1523-1534)
Benedict IX (1032-1048)	Paul III (1534-1549), he was sometimes referred to as the "Borgia brother-in-law".
Benedict X (1058-1060)	Pius IV (1559-1565)

The Borgia and Medici Popes (right) and Counts of Tusculum (left) (almost) exactly 500 years earlier.

The English historian E. Johnson (1842-1901) had already discovered that Christianity is not as old as it is written in the history books. According to his research, all early Christian writings, including the Bible, only were created in the period around 1500 and later, and thus Christianity as well [Johnson 1894 and 1904].

In fact, it was not until the Council of Trent (1545-1563) that the Latin text of the Bible version "Vulgata" was determined by the Catholic Church to be the authoritative text of the Bible. According to official history, this Bible text was written around 400, more than 1100 years earlier. Jerome (347-420) is said to be the author, who translated the Greek text of the Old Testament into Latin and revised an older translation for the New Testament.

"Jerome" (Ἱερώνυμος) is Greek and means "Holy Name". This is indeed a most fitting name for the author of the Holy Scripture!

The true beginning of our era

Christianity is known to have adopted much from older traditions.

E.g. Christmas = Winter solstice.

E.g. Easter = Passover, which goes back to the exodus of the people of Israel from Egypt, 1313 years before.

"Christ our Passover Lamb has been sacrificed."
(1 Corinthians)

Jesus Christ allegedly was crucified at the time of the sacrifice of the Passover lambs (Gospel of John).

According to the author's discoveries, the beginning of our era was also taken over from older traditions (see Hack #8 p. 171).

The true beginning of our era: The Exodus of the People of Israel from Egypt. Moses climbs Mount Sinai and God makes the covenant with the people.

40 years later: Jesus (from the Old Testament) crosses the Jordan River with the Ark of the Covenant: Entry into the Promised Land.

Between the Exodus from Egypt and the alleged birth of Jesus Christ, there are 1313 made-up years.

The Jesus of the Old Testament is called "Joshua" today only in Bible versions that go back to the Latin Bible. A name change to distinguish him from the newly created (doubled) Jesus of the New Testament.

The model for the Jesus Christ of the New Testament lived 1000 years later, in the 11th century:

The Eastern Roman Emperor Anastasios (English: "The Resurrected One", a synonym for Jesus Christ).

Alexander the Great

Alexander the Great has characteristics of the Old Testament Jesus and the New Testament Jesus. He conquers many countries like the old one, but only becomes 33 years old like the new one. The ascent to heaven is an artistic motif associated with both Alexander and Jesus.

The author has proposed in [Arndt 2020/2, p. 185 ff.] a re-dating of the Babylonian eclipse accounts, 1136 years later than in the official history (see p. 164-169). For example, the much-discussed solar eclipse of the alleged 15 April 136 BC actually occurred on 7 April 1000.

Fig. 128: Alexander the Great on a medallion from the 3rd century AD

Alexander the Great was born in 356 BC according to official history. Taking this re-dating into account, his birth was in 781 (-355 + 1136 = 781).

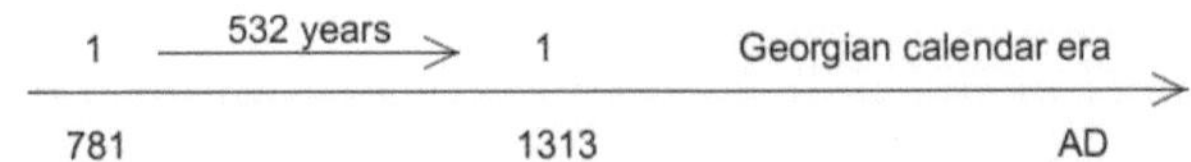

Fig. 129: The Georgian calendar era (in Georgia in the Caucasus) begins in 781

In the year 781 also begins

1) the Georgian calendar (in Georgia in the Caucasus),
2) the matching year count for Roman eclipse reports of the time until 395 AD (division of the Roman Empire) [Arndt 2020/2, p. 81 ff.] (see p. 163), and
3) plus three years (784) the Easter dates fitting for Rome after the so-called Easter Controversy [Arndt 2021/2, p. 108 ff.].

For the eclipse reports of the 5th - 6th century (after the division of the Roman Empire in 395), on the other hand, there are better fitting actual eclipses 521 years later than in the official history (see p. 163).

If the eclipse reports are thus placed in the correct chronological order, this also results in a correct placement of the historical events that are linked to these eclipse reports in the historical sources.

It has already been shown that it can be stated that Anastasios I, who according to official history became Roman Emperor in Constantinople in 491, actually took office in 1012 (see p. 176):

521 + 491 = 1012

The year 1012, which, starting from 521, corresponds to the year 491, is also identical with the year 231, starting from 781 (or 228, starting from 784). At that time Severus Alexander was Roman Emperor in Rome.

Babylonian eclipse accounts match 1136 years better, as mentioned earlier. Babylonian history is inseparable from Greek history.

Based on the year 1136, not only is the birth of Alexander the Great in 781, but also the beginning of the Seleucid era (conventionally 311 BC) in 825.

The year 825 also marks the beginning of the Indian Malayalam calendar (see [Arndt 2020/2, p. 206 ff.]).

When did Emperor Constantine the Great live?

According to official history, there were Roman emperors named Constantine, Constans and Constantius in both the fourth and fifth centuries.

Constantius I and II, Constantine I and II, and Constans I ruled in the fourth century AD, according to official history. Constantine III, Constans II as well as Constantius III ruled in the fifth century.

There are also emperors named Valentinian, Theodosius, Julian and Jovian/Jovinus in both the fourth and the first half of the fifth century.

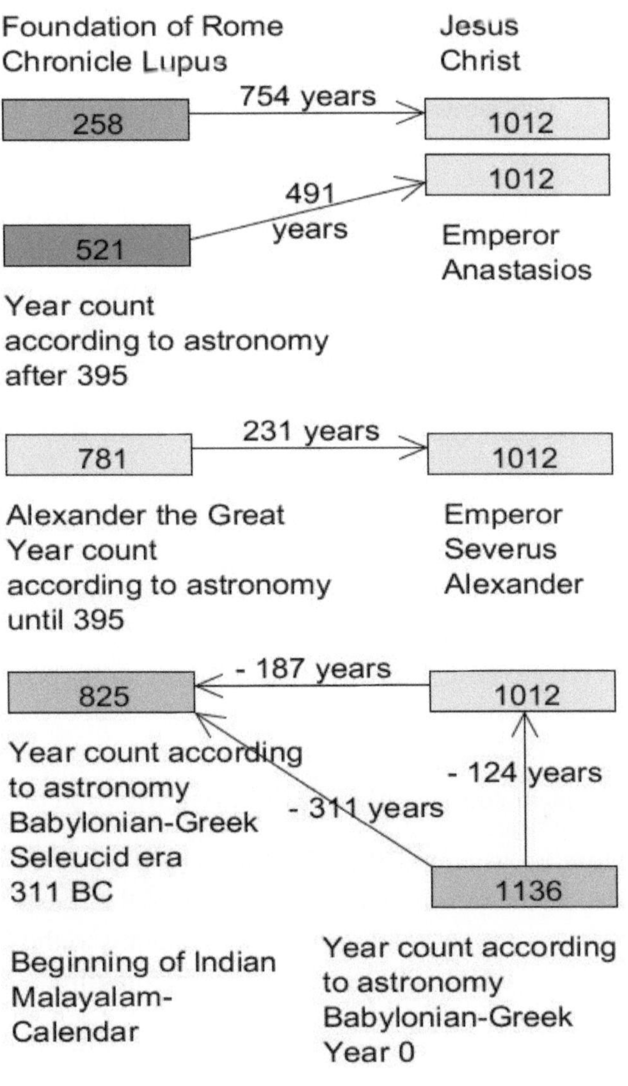

Fig. 130: The foundations of the new chronology

Here, of course, the suspicion of duplication of real persons in literature immediately arises.

Constantine I is also known as "the Great" - Constantine III is rather "the Little".

Although Constantine III was proclaimed emperor in Britain in the same way as Constantine I, he was in fact only usurper and later co-emperor in the west of the Roman Empire. According to some authors, he was the grandfather of King Arthur.

The new chronological order with the help of astronomy, specifically the eclipse reports, places Constantine III (emperor from 407 - 411) in the first half of the 10th century:

521 + 407 = 928

He would thus not be the third Constantine, but the first, since Constantine I (Emperor from 306 - 337) lived later according to the re-dating of the eclipse reports (year count according to astronomy until 395):

781 + 306 = 1087

The numeration is, of course, only an arbitrary attribution of official history.

It must therefore be assumed that the foundation of Constantinople and other heroic deeds attributed to the Constantine of the fourth century (306 - 337), insofar as they are not made-up, actually belong to the Constantine of the fifth century (407 - 411), who actually lived before him.

Maybe Constantine (306 - 337) and the other doubles did not even exist?

The official history can't explain it: Emperor Constantine had the Arch of Constantine (Arcus Constantini) built in Rome. This triumphal arch was extended by the emperors Hadrian (117 - 138) and Marcus Aurelius (161 - 180), and possibly also by Trajan (98 - 117).

According to official history, however, these three emperors reigned before Constantine.

With the described re-dating of the eclipse reports and the historical events associated with them, Emperor Constantine III (now the First!) is placed in the time of Emperor Trajan.

Fig. 131: The Arch of Constantine in Rome in 1742

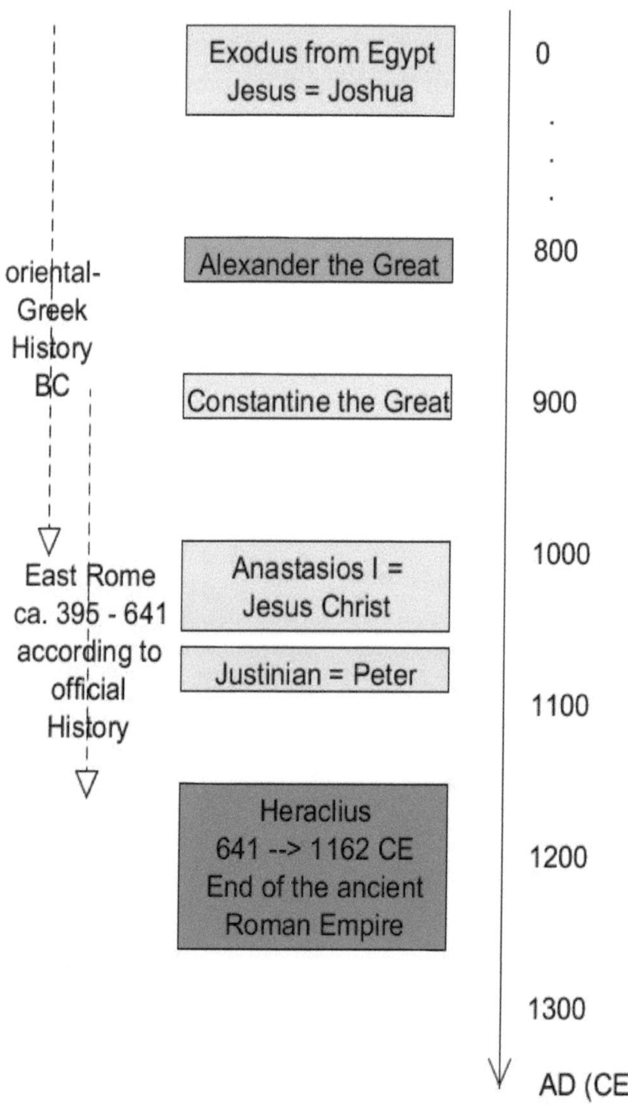

Fig. 132: New chronology Oriental-Greek-Roman tradition; on the right, the timeline of our calendar era (Common Era)

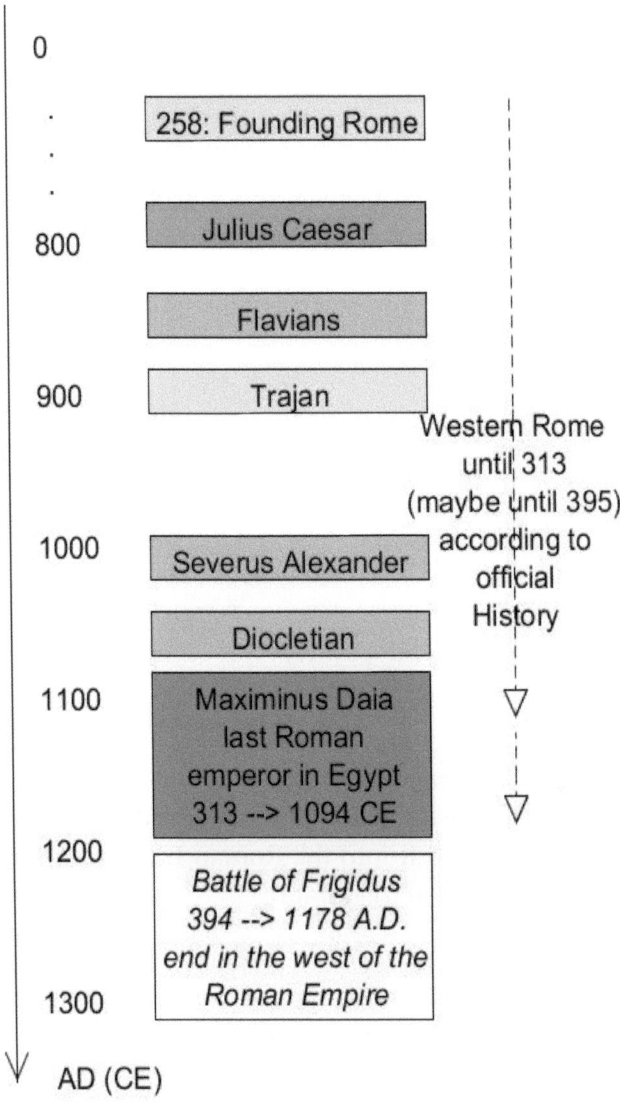

Fig. 133: New Chronology (Western) Roman Tradition

A new chronology

(see Fig. 132/133 on p. 198/199)

The dating of Constantine the Great at the beginning of the 10th century CE (Common Era) connects the emperors of the Flavian dynasty of the first century (Vespasian, Titus and Domitian) with the emperors of the Flavian dynasty of the 4th/5th century (Constantius I, Constantine I, etc.). Official history here arbitrarily separates the emperors of the same dynasty by several centuries.

Fig. 134: Emperor Vespasian (69-79)

Fig. 135: Emperor Constantine I. (306-337)

The Flavian Emperor Vespasian (69-79) had annexed Byzantium, later Constantinople, and incorporated it into the Roman Empire. Before that, it had been a free city (civitas libera et foederata).

Without this chronological correction, there are 209 years between the death of Domitian in 96 and the elevation of Constantius to emperor in 305. 311 years pass between Domitian and Constantine III in 407.

The Germanic Vandals minted coins with the image of Vespasian, which are attributed to the 5th century. This only makes sense with the proposed new chronology.

Chinese written sources mention envoys from the Roman Empire who are attributed to the 2nd century. Roman gold coins found in China, however, are attributed to Roman emperors of the 5th century.

The last Roman emperors attested hieroglyphically in Egypt are Maximian (285-310), Galerius (293-311) and Maximinus Daia (305-313).

But neither Constantius I nor Constantine I and successors left any traces in Egypt.

This corresponds to the re-dating of these emperors, who then in reality ruled parallel to the emperors of the second and third centuries attested in Egypt.

According to the re-dating, shifted by 781 - 784 years according to the eclipse reports, Maximinus Daia reigned at the end of the 11th century.

Does Roman history already end here, around 1100?

Or does it continue with emperors named Constantine, Constantius, Constans etc. (if these are real names at all) for a few more decades?

The definitive end of Western Roman antiquity is marked by the Battle of Frigidus, one of the greatest battles of the Roman Empire, with the practical annihilation of the Western army. At the time of the battle, the sources (Zosimus) mention a total eclipse of the sun.

This battle is recorded on 5-6/9/ 394, a few months before the final division of the Roman Empire in 395. My dating of the eclipse and thus of the battle is one week later, on 13/9/ 1178, with a difference of 784 years to the dating of official history.

By the way, the official history has nothing adequate to offer for the solar eclipse during the Battle of Frigidus as recorded in the sources and dates the eclipse on 20/11/ 393.

Fig. 136: The Battle of the Frigidus in 394

Our era (Common Era) therefore does not begin with the birth of Jesus Christ, who was later crucified according to Christianity, but with the Exodus of the people of Israel from Egypt and God's covenant with Moses and the people (currently dated to 1313 BC).

The Roman/Byzantine Emperor Anastastios I (redated in the 11th century CE) plays the role of the re-appearing Jesus as Christ (Messiah), the Resurrected One, sometimes also seen as the Anti-Christ.

Peter, his successor on the imperial throne with the imperial name Justinian I, founded the Orthodox Church.

In the 12th/13th century CE (Common Era), the ancient Roman Empire ends both in the West and in the East or transitions into the medieval kingdoms.

Later, a prolonged history is retroactively constructed in the national kingdoms of Europe, with all the constructed medieval lists of kings that the author analysed and described in his book "The Well-Structured History"[Arndt 2020/4] (see Hack #1).

Fig. 137: Europe in 1190 according to official history

HISTORY
YOU HAVE BEEN
HACKED !

List of figures

All graphics and tables in the book were created by the author of this book.

The illustrations of the solar and lunar eclipses are from the website http://eclipse.gsfc.nasa.gov and are in the public domain.

All other illustrations in the book are in the public domain and come from wikipedia.

Bibliography

Althoff, Gerd (2005): Die Ottonen. Königsherrschaft ohne Staat; Stuttgart

Arndt, Mario (2010): Lupus Protospatharius Barensis und ein Versuch der Rekonstruktion der Chronologie; http://de.geschichte-chronologie.de/index.php?option=com_content&view=article&id=116:lupus-protospatharius-barensis-und-ein-versuch-der-rekonstruktion-der-chronologie&catid=4:2008-11-13-21-59-32&Itemid=92

Arndt, Mario (2010/1): Die Systeme der Namen der römisch-deutschen und französischen Könige des Hochmittelalters: http://de.geschichte-chronologie.de/index.php?option=com_content&view=article&id=112:die-systeme-der-namen-der-roemisch-deutschen-und-franzoesischen-koenige-des-hochmittelalters&catid=30:2008-11-15-18-07-26&Itemid=116

Arndt, Mario (2010/2): Von den Merowingern bis zu Karl V. und darüber hinaus - die Systeme der Königsnamen: http://de.geschichte-chronologie.de/index.php?option=com_content&view=article&id=113:von-den-merowingern-bis-zu-karl-v-und-darueber-hinaus-die-systeme-der-koenigsnamen&catid=30:2008-11-15-18-07-26&Itemid=116

Arndt, Mario (2012): Das wohlstrukturierte Mittelalter; Norderstedt

Arndt, Mario (2012/2): Die wohlstrukturierte Papstliste: http://de.geschichte-chronologie.de/index.php?option=com_content&view=article&id=128:die-wohlstrukturierte-papstliste&catid=30:2008-11-15-18-07-26&Itemid=116

Arndt, Mario (2012/3): Die wohlstrukturierte Antike: http://de.geschichte-chronologie.de/index.php?option=com_content&view=article&id=127:die-wohlstrukturierte-antike&catid=29:2008-11-15-18-07-02&Itemid=115

Arndt, Mario (2020/1): Die wohlkonstruierte Chronologie; Norderstedt

Arndt, Mario (2020/2): Astronomie und Chronologiekritik; Norderstedt

Arndt, Mario (2020/3): Wer war Karl der Große wirklich?; Norderstedt

Arndt, Mario (2020/4): Die wohlstrukturierte Geschichte; Norderstedt

Arndt, Mario (2021/0): History Hacking; Norderstedt

Arndt, Mario (2021/1): Kaiser Augustus und die erfundene Antike; Norderstedt

Arndt, Mario (2021/2): Jesus Christus auf dem Kaiserthron; Norderstedt

Archiv (1900): Archiv für österreichische Geschichte, 88. Band; Wien

Assmann, Jan (2005): Das kulturelle Gedächtnis; München

Bach, Adolf (1943): Die deutschen Personennamen; Berlin

BdW (2001): Zwei Drittel der Merowinger-Urkunden sind Fälschungen in Bild der Wissenachaft 10.12.2001; http://www.wissenschaft.de/home/-/journal_content/56/12054/1181939/

Berg, Dieter (2003): Die Anjou-Plantagenets; Stuttgart

Bluer, Peter (2018): "373 – A Proof Set in Stone"; Manchester

Boll, Franz (1970): Hebdomas in: Wilhelm Kroll: Paulys Realencyklopädie der classischen Altertumswissenschaft, Band. 7.2; Stuttgart

Borst, Arno (1990): Computus. Zeit und Zahl in der Geschichte Europas;Berlin

Brenner, Wolfgang (2019): "Das deutsche Datum. Der neunte November"; Freiburg

Calvisius, Seth (1650): Opus chronologicum; Frankfurt

Conzelmann, Hans (1954): Die Mitte der Zeit. Studien zur Theologie des Lukas. Beiträge zur historischen Theologie 17. Mohr, Tübingen 7. Aufl. 1993

Curzon, Paul und McOwan Peter (2018): Computational Thinking; Berlin

Danto, Arthur C. (1965): Analytical Philosophy of History; Cambridge

Däppen, Christoph (2004): Nostradamus und Das Rätsel der Weltzeitalter; Norderstedt

Davidson, R. (2002): Der Zivilisationsprozeß; Hamburg

Demandt, Alexander (1970): Verformungstendenzen in der Überlieferung antiker Sonnen- und Mondfinsternisee in: Abhandlungen der geistes- und sozialwissenschaftlichen Klasse Nr. 7; Mainz

Devlin, Keith (2003): "Das Mathe-Gen"; München

Diacu, Florian (2005): The Lost Millenium; Toronto

Dray, William (1954): Explanatory Narrative in History, in The Philosophical Quarterly, Volume 4, Issue 14, January 1954, Pages 15–27

Dübbers, Volker (2008): Gelüftete Geheimnisse des gregorianischen Kalenders = http://www.sinossevis.de/upload1/_Gel_374ftete_Geheimnisse_des_gregorianischen_Kalenders_Mai_2008.pdf

Duncan, David Ewing (1999): The Calendar; London

Eichhoff, Seibicke und Wolffsohn (Herausgeber) (2001): Name und Gesellschaft. Soziale und historische Aspekte der Namengebung und Namenentwicklung; Mannheim

Ewig, Eugen (2006):Die Merowinger und das Frankenreich; Stuttgart

Faußner, Hans Constantin (2003): Wibald von Stablo. Erster Teil. Einführung in die Problematik; Hildesheim

Feyerabend, Paul (1986): Wider den Methodenzwang; Frankfurt

Fomenko, Anatoli (1994): Empirico-statistical analysis of narrative material and its applications to historical dating; Dordrecht

Fomenko, Anatoli (2003-2006): History: Fiction or Science; Paris/London/New York

Fried, Johannes (2016): Karl der Große; München

Fried, Johannes (1996) :Stand und Perspektiven der Mittelalterforschung am Ende des 20. Jahrhunderts; Göttingen

Fuhrmann, Horst (1988): MGH, Band 33.I., Fälschungen im Mittelalter, Teil I; München

Geuenich, Dieter (1976): Die Personennamen der Klostergemeinschaft von Fulda im fruheren Mittelalter; Munchen

Geuenich, Dieter u.a. (Herausgeber) (1997): Nomen et gens. Zur historischen Aussagekraft fruhmittelalterlicher Personennamen; Berlin

Gautschy, Rita: Eclipsecitations, http://www.gautschy.ch/~rita/archast/solec/eclipsecitations-.pdf

Gabowitsch, E. (2007): Erfundene Antike Teil 1: http://de.geschichte-chronologie.de/index.php?option=com_content&view=article&id=71:erfundene-antike-teil-1&catid=29:2008-11-15-18-07-02&Itemid=115

Gabowitsch, Eugen (2008): Die Geschichte der Geschichtsanalytik, Vortrag bei der IV. Internationalen Tagung für Geschichtsanalytik, Geschichtssalon Potsdam, Neuer Geschichtssalon Berlin, https://www.youtube.com/watch?v=R0WWiluNuBI

Gabowitsch, Eugen (2011): Chinesische Astronomie contra chinesische Geschichts-schreibung: http://de.geschichte-chronologie.de/index.php?option=com_content&view=article&id=122:chinesische-astronomie-contra-chinesische-geschichtsschreibung&catid=21:2008-11-15-18-03-39&Itemid=107

Ginzel, Friedrich Karl (1906-1914): Handbuch der mathematischen und technischen Chronologie (3 Bände); Leipzig

Goetz, Hans-Werner (1993): Die Zeit als Ordnungsfaktor in der hochmittelalterlichen Geschichtsschreibung, in Rhythmus und Saisonalität. Kongressakten des 5. Symposiums des Mediävistenverbandes in Göttingen 1993 Dilg, Peter; Keil, Gundolf; Moser, Dietz-Rüdiger [Hrsg.], Sigmaringen 1995

Grandes Chroniques de France, 15. Jahrhundert, Neuauflage in 10 Bänden (1920-1953); Paris

Grenon, Michel (2012) Charles d'Anjou; Paris

Grotefend, H. (1960): Taschenbuch der Zeitrechnung des deutschen Mittelalters und der Neuzeit; Hannover

Grundmann, Herbert (1987): Geschichtsschreibung im Mittelalter, Göttingen

Haldon, John (2007): Byzanz. Geschichte und Kultur eines Jahrtausends; Düsseldorf

Halsall, Paul (1997): Byzantine Historiography: http://legacy.fordham.edu/halsall/byzantium/texts/byzhistorio.asp

Heinsohn, Gunnar (2009): "Wie alt ist das Menschengeschlecht?"; Gräfelding

Heinsohn, Gunnar (2020): The 1st Millenium A.D. Chronology Controversy, https://www.q-mag.org/the-1st-millennium-ad-chronology-controversy.html

Herrmann, Dieter (2000):Nochmals: Gab es eine Phantomzeit in unserer Geschichte?. In: Beiträge zur Astronomiegeschichte 3. 2000, S. 211–214

Hillbrenner, Anke und Jahnz, Charlotte (2019): "Der 9. November"; Köln

Holford-Strevens, Leofranc (2008): Kleine Geschichte der Zeitrechnung und des Kalenders; Stuttgart

Hunger, Hermann und Sachs, Abraham J. (1996): Astronomical diaries and related texts from Babylonia, Vol. II. ; Wien

Ideler, Ludwig (1825/26): Handbuch der mathematischen und technischen Chronologie (2 Bände); Berlin

Illig, Heribert (1993): Das Ende des Heiligen Benedikt ? Der andere 'Vater des Abendlandes' wird auch fiktiv, in Zeitensprünge 2/93, S. 23-28

Illig, Heribert (1996): Das erfundene Mittelalter – Hat Karl der Große je gelebt?; München

Illig, Heribert (2004): Schwedens ausgemusterte Karle (aus Zeitensprünge 2/2004) = http://www.fantomzeit.de/?p=231)

Jaspert, Nikolas (2020): Von Karl dem Großen bis Kaiser Wilhelm: Die Erinnerung an vermeintliche und tatsächliche Kreuzzüge in Mittelalter und Moderne; http://archiv.ub.uni-heidelberg.de/volltextserver/16941/1/Jaspert_Von_Karl_dem_Grossen_bis_Kaiser_Wilhelm.pdf

Johnson, Edwin (1894): The Pauline Epistles

Johnson, Edwin (1904): The Rise of English Culture

Kammeier, Wilhelm (2000): Die Fälschung der deutschen Geschichte; Viöl

Knauer (2014): Das Christentum und die politische Ordnung : http://www.st-paulus-dom.info/dombibliothek/kdg/politische_ordnung.htm

Leo, Heinrich (1839): Lehrbuch der Universalgeschichte, Erster Band; Halle

Koch, Jörg (2009): "Der 9. November in der deutschen Geschichte"; Freiburg

Korth, Hans-Erdmann (2013): Der größte Irrtum der Weltgeschichte, Leipzig

Kortüm, Friedrich (1836-1837): Geschichte des Mittelalters, 2 Bände; Bern

Krieger, Karl-Friedrich (2009): Geschichte Englands 1: Von den Anfangen bis zum 15. Jahrhundert; Munchen

Krojer, Franz (2003): Die Präzision der Präzession; München

Krug, Philipp (1848): Forschungen in der alteren Geschichte Ruslands; St. Petersburg

Kugler, Franz Xaver (1907): Sternkunde und Sterndienst in Babel, Band 1: Entwickelung der babylonischen Planetenkunde von ihren Anfängen bis auf Christus; Münster

Kuhn, Thomas S. (1996): Die Struktur wissenschaftlicher Revolutionen; Berlin

Kuzenkov, Pavel (2006): How old is the world ? The Byzantine era and its rivals = http://www.wra1th.plus.com/byzcong/comms/Kuzenkov_paper.pdf

Le Goff, Jacques (1965): Das Hochmittelalter; Frankfurt

LexMA = Lexikon des Mittelalters (2002); München

Lietzmann, Hans und Aland, Kurt (1956): Zeitrechnung der römischen Kaiserzeit, des Mittelalters und der Neuzeit; Berlin

Lilie Ralph-Johannes (2003): Byzanz. Das zweite Rom; Berlin

Maier, Hans (2000): Die christliche Zeitrechnung; Freiburg i. B.

McGough, Richard Amiel (2006); "The Bible Wheel"; Yakima

Meisegeier, Michael (2017): Der frühchristliche Kirchenbau – das Produkt eines Chronologiefehlers; Norderstedt

Mitterauer, Michael (1993): Ahnen und Heilige. Namengebung in der europaischen Geschichte; Munchen

MGH (1986): Fälschungen im Mittelalter. Internationaler Kongress der Monumenta Germaniae Historica, München, 16.-19. September 1986; Hannover

Monumenta Germaniae Historica, entsprechende Einträge/MGH digital = http://bsbdmgh.bsb.lrz-muenchen.de/dmgh_new/

Morrison, L. und Stephenson, F. R. (2004): Historical Values of the Earth's Clock Error Delta T and the Calculation of Eclipses in: J. Hist. Astron., Vol. 35 Part 3, August 2004, No. 120, S. 327-336

NASA (2021): NASA Eclipse Website, http://eclipse.gsfc.nasa.gov/eclipse.html

Neugebauer, Otto (1989): Chronography in ethiopic sources; Wien

Newton, Robert R. (1970): Ancient Astronomical Observations and the Accelerations of the Earth and Moon; Baltimore/London

Newton, Robert R. (1972): Medieval Chronicles and the Acceleration of the Earth; Baltimore/London

Newton, Robert R. (1977): The Crime of Claudius Ptolemy; Baltimore/London

Norwich, John J. (2006): Byzanz. Aufstieg und Fall eines Weltreichs; Berlin

Oppolzer, Theodor (1887): Canon der Finsternisse; Wien

Petavius, Dionysius (1633): Rationarium temporum; Paris

Petit, Joseph (1900): Charles de Valois; 1900

Pfister, Christoph (2019): Die Matrix der alten Geschichte; Norderstedt

Popper, Karl R. (1935): Die Logik der Forschung; Wien

Ranke (1854): Abhandlungen der Berliner Akademie; Berlin

Richards, E. G. (1998): Mapping Time. The Calendar and its History; Oxford

Sarre, François de (2013), "Mais où est donc passé le Moyen Âge"; Paris (Franz.)

Scaliger, Joseph J. (1629): De emendatione temporum; Genf

Schmale, Franz-Josef (1985): Funktion und Formen mittelalterlicher Geschichtsschreibung. Eine Einführung, Darmstadt

Schmidt (2020): https://groups.google.com/group/de.sci.astronomie/msg/32118a406cad2ba3?hl=de

Schneidmüller, Bernd und Weinfurter, Stefan (2003): Die deutschen Herrscher des Mittelalters; München

Seibicke, Wilfried (2008): Die Personennamen im Deutschen; Berlin

Serrade, Gérard (1998): Leere Zeiten; Berlin

Starke, Ronald (2013): Niemand hat an der Uhr gedreht!; München; http://www.differenz-verlag.de/starke-illig/BuchNeu2013Mai21.pdf

Steiner, Benjamin (2008): Die Ordnung der Geschichte: Historische Tabellenwerke in der Frühen Neuzeit; Köln, Weimar, Wien

Stephenson, F. Richard (1997): Historical Eclipses and Earth's Rotation; Cambridge

Stern, Fritz u.a. (1994): "Der 9. November"; München

Tabarai: La Chronique, De Salomon à la chute des Sassanides, Éditions Actes Sud; Arles

Topper, Uwe (1998): Die große Aktion; Tübingen

Unzicker, Alexander (2010): Vom Urknall zum Durchknall. Die absurde Jagd nach der Weltformel; Heidelberg

Vollemaere, A.L. (2012): Apocalypse Maya 2012 (Foutaise ou science?); (Franz.)

Von den Brincken, Anna-Dorothee (2000): Historische Chronologie des Abendlandes; Stuttgart, Berlin, Köln

Weinfurter, Stefan (2015): Karl der Große; München

Weinreb, Friedrich (1986): Zahl-Zeichen-Wort, Weiler

Wiemer, Hans-Ulrich (2018): Theoderich der Große; München

wikipedia = http://de.wikipedia.org

Wing, Jeannette M. (2006): "Computational Thinking" in COMMUNICATIONS OF THE ACM, March 2006/Vol. 49, No. 3; https://www.cs.cmu.edu/~15110-s13/Wing06-ct.pdf